TAP
DANCING
THROUGH
LIFE

Published by Advantage, Charleston, South Carolina.
Member of Advantage Media Group.

ADVANTAGE is a registered trademark and the Advantage colophon is a trademark of Advantage Media Group, Inc.

Printed in the United States of America.

ISBN: 978-1-59932-086-1
LCCN: 2008933624

Most Advantage Media Group titles are available at special quantity discounts for bulk purchases for sales promotions, premiums, fundraising, and educational use. Special versions or book excerpts can also be created to fit specific needs.

For more information, please write: Special Markets, Advantage Media Group, P.O. Box 272, Charleston, SC 29402 or call 1.866.775.1696.

TAP DANCING THROUGH LIFE

THROUGH

LIFE

DAILY SUCCESS JOURNAL

FINDING YOUR PERSONAL RHYTHM and **ACHIEVING THE LIFE OF YOUR DREAMS**

VAL GOKENBACH

Advantage®

DEDICATION

My wonderful family Rick, Rick, Nikki, Casey and Abigail
I love you all so much!!!!!

INTRODUCTION

Welcome back to the world of Tap Dancing Through Life and your journey to the realization of a fulfilled life. This personal journal is a valuable tool to use to help you organize your thoughts and keep your progress on track. Vince Lombardi said "The quality of a person's life is in direct proportion to their commitment to excellence, regardless of their chose field of endeavor." The intent of this journal is to help you identify your uniqueness and channel your individual thoughts to help you achieve whatever you feel is exciting and rewarding in your life.

There are three major OBJECTIVES to this journal:

1. To allow you to introspectively review your progress, discuss your disappointments and charter new strategies to keep you moving in a positive direction.

2. To help you learn to live day by day and optimize the time you have in the present rather than worry about the future.

3. To introduce you to the power of journaling as a tool to help you achieve the life of your dreams.

"It is a funny thing about life; if you refuse to accept anything but the best, you very often get it." —Somerset Maugham

Time to get moving—Good luck!!

WHAT HAVE WE LEARNED?

In the book you learned several valuable lessons that we will briefly review. This refresher may help you reconnect to some of the feelings and insights that you realized while you were moving through all of the exercises to find out more about yourself.

Personal Rhythms

Everything in life falls into a pattern of rhythm that repeats itself and is responsible for the manifestation of the outcomes of our life. Habits, thought patterns and physiological functions must remain in a balanced rhythm if we are going to be healthy. We have all experienced times in our lives where the loss of our rhythms have contributed to problems. Catastrophes, life changes, illness, role and job expectations are a few examples of these. Personal choices to eliminate healthy rhythms from our lives can also affect our lives such as not exercising, not sleeping well or not eating a well balanced diet. You had the opportunity in the book to identify those rhythms and make positive changes. This journal will help you chart your daily progress.

Self-Knowledge

Understanding yourself and knowing what you want to achieve is the first step to developing plans for your future. In the book you had the opportunity to explore your value system and to develop goals for your life. Take a moment to write those goals down to provide a reference for your journaling.

PERSONAL GOALS

Goal #1 _____
_____
_____

Goal #2 _____
_____
_____

Goal#3 _____
_____
_____

Goal#4 _____
_____
_____

Power of Positive Thinking

It has been said that what calls us to action in our lives is desire, but what helps us achieve our goals is the belief in ourselves that we can accomplish the goal. This belief in ourselves is called self-efficacy. If we believe we can achieve it, then we are always right. If we believe we cannot achieve it, we are also always right. So, the choice becomes yours. "I have learned from experience that the greater part of our happiness or misery depends on our dispositions and not on our circumstances." Martha Washington

More and more, research is beginning to unlock the science behind the power of positive thought as well as the psychological and physical problems associated with chronic negative thought. You have had the opportunity to identify your thought patterns in the exercises in the book. The structure of this journal will provide you the opportunity to focus on your positive thoughts and analyze the origins of your negative thoughts.

Stress and Living Day By Day

Very simply, the term stress refers to any demands either physical or emotional placed on the body. Stress in of itself is not necessarily bad for us if we learn to control it. In fact, stress is the body's normal mechanism to kick up our metabolism and energy to meet the body's demands. It readies us for the emotional and physical challenges we face throughout our lives. Some degree of stress is an advantage that peaks our performance by heightening awareness and stimulating the body. The problem with stress is the concern that we, as a society, are under continuous pressure, which keeps us in an overloaded state for protracted periods of time. This continued pressure is what leads to emotional fatigue and disease.

Another phenomenon with stress is that 99 percent of it is nothing more than personal unrealistic fears that never manifest in our lives. This is the practice of worrying. Ester Hicks, in her writings about the law of attraction stated that "Worrying is the body's way of using its own energy to manifest what we don't want in our lives." In the book we identified your stressors and also worked on a technique called the meditation moment to help you handle episodic stress. Another positive approach to handling stress is to live day by day rather than worry about the future. The journal will help you channel your thoughts to focus on the events of the day rather than the unknown future.

Trifecta of Health: Exercise, Sleep and Nutrition

Positive personal habits are vital to your health. In the book we devoted a chapter to each one of these topics. As you begin your journaling process, be sure to focus on the goals that included your rhythms of exercise, sleep and nutrition.

ALL ABOUT JOURNALING

Journaling is a process of keeping a log of written documentation that explores personal thoughts and feelings in response to emotions, experiences, desires and challenges. The following are many benefits of journaling.

Allows for the release of frustration and anger that remains hidden during the day

Helps in the achievement of personal goals by providing updates, ideas and verification of success in written form

Allows for the blocking of sequential thinking unlocking hidden patterns and thought

Helps in the solving of complex problems by allowing the mind to clarify issues

Allows for quiet time which taps into the subconscious mind

Helps to access personal wisdom from past experiences to help meet current personal challenges

Helps to identify hidden stressors or fears that may plague the mind on a subconscious level

Helps to unlock personal creativity since there are no barriers to thought

Helps to clarify and organize personal thought rhythms and processes

Helps to provide personal insights for self-analysis

Journaling Processes

We will be using two types of journaling processes in this book which I will refer to as ***action journaling*** and ***freestyle journaling.*** I encourage you to use both types of journaling since they both have specific application to what you are trying to achieve in your life.

Action Journaling

Every day you will have the opportunity to action journal. This type of journaling is targeted to challenge your thoughts in s specific direction to allow for focused attention. The areas chosen for concentration in this journal relate back to the areas of concentration in the book and the goals you have set for your life.

The journaling topics also focus you in a positive frame and help to identify what you are grateful for.

You will be asked to answer the following questions…

What do I desire to improve my life?

What will I do to achieve the improvement?

What challenges/stressors did I face today?

What did I do or need to do tomorrow rise to the challenges?

What did I learn from today's experiences?

What am I grateful for today?

How did I today or will I tomorrow improve my personal rhythms of exercise, nutrition and sleep?

Simply think about your day and select particular feelings that arise around the topics identified and write about your successes, challenges and plans for the next day. Remember that we are focusing on living day to day with your journal. Your long term objectives have been developed when you did the exercises in the book.

Freestyle Journaling

The next page of the journal is blank and an opportunity for you to freestyle journal. Just begin writing. Write about anything you wish and place no restrictions on your thoughts. This is your opportunity to be creative and to unlock your subconscious mind to new ways of thinking. When you finish, read your entries and see if you can apply any of your thoughts to your personal improvement plan. Sometimes you will find some pearls of wisdom and sometimes you won't so don't look for anything in particular.

Weekly Review

Lastly, on every seventh day, there is an opportunity for you to review your weekly progress. This is important to provide you the opportunity to see your success and to celebrate what you have achieved.

How Often Should I Journal and When

There are no rules about journaling and the only recommendation is that you make this a regular process in your life. Just like exercise, we may not have the time to journal on a daily basis but you should try to carve out some personal time to achieve this. I designed this journal to be portable so you can keep it in a briefcase, backpack or purse and use it during downtime period through the day. Freestyle journaling is best done when you have time to decompress and let the creative thoughts flow. That may not happen on a subway or between meetings at work.

Off and Running

You now have all the information and tools to begin your journaling. Remember that "genius is the ability to reduce the complicated to the simple." C.W.Ceran. Knowing who you are, living day by day and focusing on your progress will help to channel your thoughts and compartmentalize your life! Remember *YOU CAN DO THIS!!!!!!!!!*

Date:_____   **Positive Comment:**_____

What Do I Desire To Improve In My Life Today? _____
_____
_____
_____

What Will I Do to Achieve the Imrovement? _____
_____
_____
_____

What Challenges Or Stressors Did I Face Today? _____
_____
_____
_____

What Did Or Will I Do To Rise To The Challenges? _____
_____
_____
_____

What Did I Learn from Today's Experiences? _____
_____
_____
_____

What Am I Grateful for Today? _____
_____
_____
_____

How Did I Improve My Personal Rhythms For…?

Exercise: _____

Nutrition: _____

Sleep: _____

Date:_____

Date:_____   **Positive Comment:**_____

What Do I Desire To Improve In My Life Today? _____

_____

_____

_____

What Will I Do to Achieve the Imrovement? _____

_____

_____

_____

What Challenges Or Stressors Did I Face Today? _____

_____

_____

_____

What Did Or Will I Do To Rise To The Challenges? _____

_____

_____

_____

What Did I Learn from Today's Experiences? _____

_____

_____

_____

What Am I Grateful for Today? _____

_____

_____

_____

How Did I Improve My Personal Rhythms For…?

Exercise: _____

Nutrition: _____

Sleep: _____

Date:_____

Date:_____ **Positive Comment:**_____

*What Do I Desire To Improve In My Life Today?*_____

_____

_____

_____

*What Will I Do to Achieve the Imrovement?*_____

_____

_____

_____

*What Challenges Or Stressors Did I Face Today?*_____

_____

_____

_____

*What Did Or Will I Do To Rise To The Challenges?*_____

_____

_____

_____

*What Did I Learn from Today's Experiences?*_____

_____

_____

_____

*What Am I Grateful for Today?*_____

_____

_____

_____

How Did I Improve My Personal Rhythms For…?

*Exercise:*_____

*Nutrition:*_____

*Sleep:*_____

Date:_____

Date:_____ **Positive Comment:**_____

What Do I Desire To Improve In My Life Today? _____
_____
_____
_____

What Will I Do to Achieve the Imrovement? _____
_____
_____
_____

What Challenges Or Stressors Did I Face Today? _____
_____
_____
_____

What Did Or Will I Do To Rise To The Challenges? _____
_____
_____
_____

What Did I Learn from Today's Experiences? _____
_____
_____
_____

What Am I Grateful for Today? _____
_____
_____
_____

How Did I Improve My Personal Rhythms For…?
Exercise: _____
*Nutrition:*_____
Sleep: _____

Date:_____

Date:_____   **Positive Comment:**_____

What Do I Desire To Improve In My Life Today? _____
_____
_____
_____

What Will I Do to Achieve the Imrovement? _____
_____
_____
_____

What Challenges Or Stressors Did I Face Today? _____
_____
_____
_____

What Did Or Will I Do To Rise To The Challenges? _____
_____
_____
_____

What Did I Learn from Today's Experiences? _____
_____
_____
_____

What Am I Grateful for Today? _____
_____
_____
_____

How Did I Improve My Personal Rhythms For…?

*Exercise:*_____

*Nutrition:*_____

Sleep: _____

Date:_____

Date:_____   **Positive Comment:**_____

What Do I Desire To Improve In My Life Today? _____
_____
_____
_____

What Will I Do to Achieve the Imrovement? _____
_____
_____
_____

What Challenges Or Stressors Did I Face Today? _____
_____
_____
_____

What Did Or Will I Do To Rise To The Challenges? _____
_____
_____
_____

What Did I Learn from Today's Experiences? _____
_____
_____
_____

What Am I Grateful for Today? _____
_____
_____
_____

How Did I Improve My Personal Rhythms For...?

Exercise: _____

Nutrition: _____

Sleep: _____

Date:_____

_____

_____

_____

_____

_____

_____

_____

_____

_____

_____

_____

_____

_____

WEEKLY REVIEW

Areas where I felt successful this week

_____

_____

_____

Areas that I feel I need to focus on this week

_____

_____

_____

Positive personal comment for the week

_____

_____

_____

Most valuable lesson learned this week

_____

_____

_____

Date:_____   **Positive Comment:**_____

What Do I Desire To Improve In My Life Today? _____

_____

_____

_____

What Will I Do to Achieve the Imrovement? _____

_____

_____

_____

What Challenges Or Stressors Did I Face Today? _____

_____

_____

_____

What Did Or Will I Do To Rise To The Challenges? _____

_____

_____

_____

What Did I Learn from Today's Experiences? _____

_____

_____

_____

What Am I Grateful for Today? _____

_____

_____

_____

How Did I Improve My Personal Rhythms For…?

*Exercise:*_____

*Nutrition:*_____

Sleep: _____

Date:_____

Date:_____   **Positive Comment:**_____

What Do I Desire To Improve In My Life Today? _____
_____
_____
_____

What Will I Do to Achieve the Imrovement? _____
_____
_____
_____

What Challenges Or Stressors Did I Face Today? _____
_____
_____
_____

What Did Or Will I Do To Rise To The Challenges? _____
_____
_____
_____

What Did I Learn from Today's Experiences? _____
_____
_____
_____

What Am I Grateful for Today? _____
_____
_____
_____

How Did I Improve My Personal Rhythms For…?

Exercise: _____

Nutrition: _____

Sleep: _____

Date:_____

Date:_____   **Positive Comment:**_____

What Do I Desire To Improve In My Life Today? _____
_____
_____
_____

What Will I Do to Achieve the Imrovement? _____
_____
_____
_____

What Challenges Or Stressors Did I Face Today? _____
_____
_____
_____

What Did Or Will I Do To Rise To The Challenges? _____
_____
_____
_____

What Did I Learn from Today's Experiences? _____
_____
_____
_____

What Am I Grateful for Today? _____
_____
_____
_____

How Did I Improve My Personal Rhythms For…?

*Exercise:*_____

*Nutrition:*_____

Sleep: _____

Date:_____

Date:_____   **Positive Comment:**_____

What Do I Desire To Improve In My Life Today? _____

_____

_____

_____

What Will I Do to Achieve the Imrovement? _____

_____

_____

_____

What Challenges Or Stressors Did I Face Today? _____

_____

_____

_____

What Did Or Will I Do To Rise To The Challenges? _____

_____

_____

_____

What Did I Learn from Today's Experiences? _____

_____

_____

_____

What Am I Grateful for Today? _____

_____

_____

_____

How Did I Improve My Personal Rhythms For…?

Exercise: _____

Nutrition: _____

Sleep: _____

Date:_____

_____
_____
_____
_____
_____
_____
_____
_____
_____
_____
_____
_____
_____
_____
_____
_____
_____
_____
_____
_____
_____
_____
_____
_____
_____
_____
_____
_____
_____
_____
_____
_____
_____

Date:_____ Positive Comment:_____

What Do I Desire To Improve In My Life Today? _____
_____
_____
_____

What Will I Do to Achieve the Imrovement? _____
_____
_____
_____

What Challenges Or Stressors Did I Face Today? _____
_____
_____
_____

What Did Or Will I Do To Rise To The Challenges? _____
_____
_____
_____

What Did I Learn from Today's Experiences? _____
_____
_____
_____

What Am I Grateful for Today? _____
_____
_____
_____

How Did I Improve My Personal Rhythms For…?

Exercise: _____
Nutrition: _____
Sleep: _____

Date:_____

Date:_____   **Positive Comment:**_____

What Do I Desire To Improve In My Life Today? _____
_____
_____
_____

What Will I Do to Achieve the Imrovement? _____
_____
_____
_____

What Challenges Or Stressors Did I Face Today? _____
_____
_____
_____

What Did Or Will I Do To Rise To The Challenges? _____
_____
_____
_____

What Did I Learn from Today's Experiences? _____
_____
_____
_____

What Am I Grateful for Today? _____
_____
_____
_____

How Did I Improve My Personal Rhythms For…?

Exercise: _____

*Nutrition:*_____

Sleep: _____

Date:_____

_____
_____
_____
_____
_____
_____
_____
_____
_____
_____
_____
_____
_____

WEEKLY REVIEW

Areas where I felt successful this week

_____
_____
_____

Areas that I feel I need to focus on this week

_____
_____
_____

Positive personal comment for the week

_____
_____
_____

Most valuable lesson learned this week

_____
_____
_____

Date:_____ Positive Comment:_____

What Do I Desire To Improve In My Life Today? _____
_____
_____
_____

What Will I Do to Achieve the Imrovement? _____
_____
_____
_____

What Challenges Or Stressors Did I Face Today? _____
_____
_____
_____

What Did Or Will I Do To Rise To The Challenges? _____
_____
_____
_____

What Did I Learn from Today's Experiences? _____
_____
_____
_____

What Am I Grateful for Today? _____
_____
_____
_____

How Did I Improve My Personal Rhythms For…?

*Exercise:*_____

*Nutrition:*_____

Sleep: _____

Date:_____

Date:_____   **Positive Comment:**_____

What Do I Desire To Improve In My Life Today? _____

_____

_____

_____

What Will I Do to Achieve the Imrovement? _____

_____

_____

_____

What Challenges Or Stressors Did I Face Today? _____

_____

_____

_____

What Did Or Will I Do To Rise To The Challenges? _____

_____

_____

_____

What Did I Learn from Today's Experiences? _____

_____

_____

_____

What Am I Grateful for Today? _____

_____

_____

_____

How Did I Improve My Personal Rhythms For…?

Exercise: _____

*Nutrition:*_____

Sleep: _____

Date:_____

Date:_____   **Positive Comment:**_____

What Do I Desire To Improve In My Life Today? _____

_____

_____

_____

What Will I Do to Achieve the Imrovement? _____

_____

_____

_____

What Challenges Or Stressors Did I Face Today? _____

_____

_____

_____

What Did Or Will I Do To Rise To The Challenges? _____

_____

_____

_____

What Did I Learn from Today's Experiences? _____

_____

_____

_____

What Am I Grateful for Today? _____

_____

_____

_____

How Did I Improve My Personal Rhythms For…?

*Exercise:*_____

*Nutrition:*_____

Sleep: _____

Date:_____

Date:_____   **Positive Comment:**_____

What Do I Desire To Improve In My Life Today? _____
_____
_____
_____

What Will I Do to Achieve the Imrovement? _____
_____
_____
_____

What Challenges Or Stressors Did I Face Today? _____
_____
_____
_____

What Did Or Will I Do To Rise To The Challenges? _____
_____
_____
_____

What Did I Learn from Today's Experiences? _____
_____
_____
_____

What Am I Grateful for Today? _____
_____
_____
_____

How Did I Improve My Personal Rhythms For…?
*Exercise:*_____
*Nutrition:*_____
Sleep: _____

Date:_____

Date:_____   **Positive Comment:**_____

What Do I Desire To Improve In My Life Today? _____
_____
_____
_____

What Will I Do to Achieve the Imrovement? _____
_____
_____
_____

What Challenges Or Stressors Did I Face Today? _____
_____
_____
_____

What Did Or Will I Do To Rise To The Challenges? _____
_____
_____
_____

What Did I Learn from Today's Experiences? _____
_____
_____
_____

What Am I Grateful for Today? _____
_____
_____
_____

How Did I Improve My Personal Rhythms For…?

*Exercise:*_____

*Nutrition:*_____

Sleep: _____

Date:_____

Date:_____   **Positive Comment:**_____

What Do I Desire To Improve In My Life Today? _____
_____
_____
_____

What Will I Do to Achieve the Imrovement? _____
_____
_____
_____

What Challenges Or Stressors Did I Face Today? _____
_____
_____
_____

What Did Or Will I Do To Rise To The Challenges? _____
_____
_____
_____

What Did I Learn from Today's Experiences? _____
_____
_____
_____

What Am I Grateful for Today? _____
_____
_____
_____

How Did I Improve My Personal Rhythms For…?

Exercise: _____

Nutrition: _____

Sleep: _____

Date:_____

_____

_____

_____

_____

_____

_____

_____

_____

_____

_____

_____

_____

WEEKLY REVIEW

Areas where I felt successful this week

_____

_____

_____

Areas that I feel I need to focus on this week

_____

_____

_____

Positive personal comment for the week

_____

_____

_____

Most valuable lesson learned this week

_____

_____

_____

Date:_____   **Positive Comment:**_____

What Do I Desire To Improve In My Life Today? _____
_____
_____
_____

What Will I Do to Achieve the Imrovement? _____
_____
_____
_____

What Challenges Or Stressors Did I Face Today? _____
_____
_____
_____

What Did Or Will I Do To Rise To The Challenges? _____
_____
_____
_____

What Did I Learn from Today's Experiences? _____
_____
_____
_____

What Am I Grateful for Today? _____
_____
_____
_____

How Did I Improve My Personal Rhythms For…?

*Exercise:*_____

*Nutrition:*_____

Sleep: _____

Date:_____

Date:_____   **Positive Comment:**_____

What Do I Desire To Improve In My Life Today? _____
_____
_____
_____

What Will I Do to Achieve the Imrovement? _____
_____
_____
_____
_____

What Challenges Or Stressors Did I Face Today? _____
_____
_____
_____

What Did Or Will I Do To Rise To The Challenges? _____
_____
_____
_____

What Did I Learn from Today's Experiences? _____
_____
_____
_____

What Am I Grateful for Today? _____
_____
_____
_____

How Did I Improve My Personal Rhythms For…?

*Exercise:*_____

*Nutrition:*_____

Sleep: _____

Date:_____

Date:_____   **Positive Comment:**_____

What Do I Desire To Improve In My Life Today? _____

_____

_____

_____

What Will I Do to Achieve the Imrovement? _____

_____

_____

_____

What Challenges Or Stressors Did I Face Today? _____

_____

_____

_____

What Did Or Will I Do To Rise To The Challenges? _____

_____

_____

_____

What Did I Learn from Today's Experiences? _____

_____

_____

_____

What Am I Grateful for Today? _____

_____

_____

_____

How Did I Improve My Personal Rhythms For…?

*Exercise:*_____

*Nutrition:*_____

Sleep: _____

Date:_____

Date:_____   **Positive Comment:**_____

What Do I Desire To Improve In My Life Today? _____

_____

_____

_____

What Will I Do to Achieve the Imrovement? _____

_____

_____

_____

What Challenges Or Stressors Did I Face Today? _____

_____

_____

_____

What Did Or Will I Do To Rise To The Challenges? _____

_____

_____

_____

What Did I Learn from Today's Experiences? _____

_____

_____

_____

What Am I Grateful for Today? _____

_____

_____

_____

How Did I Improve My Personal Rhythms For…?

*Exercise:*_____

*Nutrition:*_____

Sleep: _____

Date:_____

_____
_____
_____
_____
_____
_____
_____
_____
_____
_____
_____
_____
_____
_____
_____
_____
_____
_____
_____
_____
_____
_____
_____
_____
_____
_____
_____
_____
_____
_____
_____
_____
_____
_____

Date:_____   **Positive Comment:**_____

*What Do I Desire To Improve In My Life Today?*_____

_____

_____

_____

*What Will I Do to Achieve the Imrovement?*_____

_____

_____

_____

*What Challenges Or Stressors Did I Face Today?*_____

_____

_____

_____

*What Did Or Will I Do To Rise To The Challenges?*_____

_____

_____

_____

*What Did I Learn from Today's Experiences?*_____

_____

_____

_____

*What Am I Grateful for Today?*_____

_____

_____

_____

How Did I Improve My Personal Rhythms For…?

*Exercise:*_____

*Nutrition:*_____

*Sleep:*_____

Date:_____

Date:_____ **Positive Comment:**_____

What Do I Desire To Improve In My Life Today? _____

_____

_____

_____

What Will I Do to Achieve the Imrovement? _____

_____

_____

_____

What Challenges Or Stressors Did I Face Today? _____

_____

_____

_____

What Did Or Will I Do To Rise To The Challenges? _____

_____

_____

_____

What Did I Learn from Today's Experiences? _____

_____

_____

_____

What Am I Grateful for Today? _____

_____

_____

_____

How Did I Improve My Personal Rhythms For…?

Exercise: _____

*Nutrition:*_____

Sleep: _____

Date:_____

_____

_____

_____

_____

_____

_____

_____

_____

_____

_____

_____

_____

WEEKLY REVIEW

Areas where I felt successful this week

_____

_____

_____

Areas that I feel I need to focus on this week

_____

_____

_____

Positive personal comment for the week

_____

_____

_____

Most valuable lesson learned this week

_____

_____

_____

Date:_____   **Positive Comment:**_____

What Do I Desire To Improve In My Life Today? _____
_____
_____
_____

What Will I Do to Achieve the Imrovement? _____
_____
_____
_____

What Challenges Or Stressors Did I Face Today? _____
_____
_____
_____

What Did Or Will I Do To Rise To The Challenges? _____
_____
_____
_____

What Did I Learn from Today's Experiences? _____
_____
_____
_____

What Am I Grateful for Today? _____
_____
_____
_____

How Did I Improve My Personal Rhythms For…?

*Exercise:*_____
*Nutrition:*_____
Sleep: _____

Date:_____

_____
_____
_____
_____
_____
_____
_____
_____
_____
_____
_____
_____
_____
_____
_____
_____
_____
_____
_____
_____
_____
_____
_____
_____
_____
_____
_____
_____
_____
_____
_____

Date:_____   **Positive Comment:**_____

What Do I Desire To Improve In My Life Today? _____
_____
_____
_____

What Will I Do to Achieve the Imrovement? _____
_____
_____
_____

What Challenges Or Stressors Did I Face Today? _____
_____
_____
_____

What Did Or Will I Do To Rise To The Challenges? _____
_____
_____
_____

What Did I Learn from Today's Experiences? _____
_____
_____
_____

What Am I Grateful for Today? _____
_____
_____
_____

How Did I Improve My Personal Rhythms For…?

*Exercise:*_____

*Nutrition:*_____

Sleep: _____

Date:_____

Date:_____   **Positive Comment:**_____

What Do I Desire To Improve In My Life Today? _____

_____

_____

_____

What Will I Do to Achieve the Imrovement? _____

_____

_____

_____

What Challenges Or Stressors Did I Face Today? _____

_____

_____

_____

What Did Or Will I Do To Rise To The Challenges? _____

_____

_____

_____

What Did I Learn from Today's Experiences? _____

_____

_____

_____

What Am I Grateful for Today? _____

_____

_____

_____

How Did I Improve My Personal Rhythms For…?

*Exercise:*_____

*Nutrition:*_____

Sleep: _____

Date:_____

Date:_____   **Positive Comment:**_____

What Do I Desire To Improve In My Life Today? _____

_____

_____

_____

What Will I Do to Achieve the Imrovement? _____

_____

_____

_____

What Challenges Or Stressors Did I Face Today? _____

_____

_____

_____

What Did Or Will I Do To Rise To The Challenges? _____

_____

_____

_____

What Did I Learn from Today's Experiences? _____

_____

_____

_____

What Am I Grateful for Today? _____

_____

_____

_____

How Did I Improve My Personal Rhythms For…?

*Exercise:*_____

*Nutrition:*_____

Sleep: _____

Date:_____

Date:_____   **Positive Comment:**_____

What Do I Desire To Improve In My Life Today? _____
_____
_____
_____

What Will I Do to Achieve the Imrovement? _____
_____
_____
_____

What Challenges Or Stressors Did I Face Today? _____
_____
_____
_____

What Did Or Will I Do To Rise To The Challenges? _____
_____
_____
_____

What Did I Learn from Today's Experiences? _____
_____
_____
_____

What Am I Grateful for Today? _____
_____
_____
_____

How Did I Improve My Personal Rhythms For…?

*Exercise:*_____

*Nutrition:*_____

Sleep: _____

Date:_____

Date:_____   **Positive Comment:**_____

What Do I Desire To Improve In My Life Today? _____

_____

_____

_____

What Will I Do to Achieve the Imrovement? _____

_____

_____

_____

What Challenges Or Stressors Did I Face Today? _____

_____

_____

_____

What Did Or Will I Do To Rise To The Challenges? _____

_____

_____

_____

What Did I Learn from Today's Experiences? _____

_____

_____

_____

What Am I Grateful for Today? _____

_____

_____

_____

How Did I Improve My Personal Rhythms For…?

*Exercise:*_____

*Nutrition:*_____

Sleep: _____

Date:_____

_____

_____

_____

_____

_____

_____

_____

_____

_____

_____

_____

_____

WEEKLY REVIEW

Areas where I felt successful this week

_____

_____

_____

Areas that I feel I need to focus on this week

_____

_____

_____

Positive personal comment for the week

_____

_____

_____

Most valuable lesson learned this week

_____

_____

_____

Date:_____ **Positive Comment:**_____

What Do I Desire To Improve In My Life Today? _____
_____
_____
_____

What Will I Do to Achieve the Imrovement? _____
_____
_____
_____

What Challenges Or Stressors Did I Face Today? _____
_____
_____
_____

What Did Or Will I Do To Rise To The Challenges? _____
_____
_____
_____

What Did I Learn from Today's Experiences? _____
_____
_____
_____

What Am I Grateful for Today? _____
_____
_____
_____

How Did I Improve My Personal Rhythms For…?

*Exercise:*_____

*Nutrition:*_____

Sleep: _____

Date:_____

Date:_____   **Positive Comment:**_____

What Do I Desire To Improve In My Life Today? _____
_____
_____
_____

What Will I Do to Achieve the Imrovement? _____
_____
_____
_____

What Challenges Or Stressors Did I Face Today? _____
_____
_____
_____

What Did Or Will I Do To Rise To The Challenges? _____
_____
_____
_____

What Did I Learn from Today's Experiences? _____
_____
_____
_____

What Am I Grateful for Today? _____
_____
_____
_____

How Did I Improve My Personal Rhythms For...?

*Exercise:*_____

*Nutrition:*_____

Sleep: _____

Date:_____

Date:_____   **Positive Comment:**_____

What Do I Desire To Improve In My Life Today? _____

_____

_____

_____

What Will I Do to Achieve the Imrovement? _____

_____

_____

_____

What Challenges Or Stressors Did I Face Today? _____

_____

_____

_____

What Did Or Will I Do To Rise To The Challenges? _____

_____

_____

_____

What Did I Learn from Today's Experiences? _____

_____

_____

_____

What Am I Grateful for Today? _____

_____

_____

_____

How Did I Improve My Personal Rhythms For...?

*Exercise:*_____

*Nutrition:*_____

Sleep: _____

Date:_____

Date:_____   **Positive Comment:**_____

What Do I Desire To Improve In My Life Today? _____

_____

_____

_____

What Will I Do to Achieve the Imrovement? _____

_____

_____

_____

_____

What Challenges Or Stressors Did I Face Today? _____

_____

_____

_____

What Did Or Will I Do To Rise To The Challenges? _____

_____

_____

_____

What Did I Learn from Today's Experiences? _____

_____

_____

_____

What Am I Grateful for Today? _____

_____

_____

_____

How Did I Improve My Personal Rhythms For…?

*Exercise:*_____

*Nutrition:*_____

Sleep: _____

Date:_____

_____

_____

_____

_____

_____

_____

_____

_____

_____

_____

_____

_____

_____

_____

_____

_____

_____

_____

_____

_____

_____

_____

_____

_____

_____

_____

_____

_____

_____

_____

_____

_____

_____

_____

_____

Date:_____   **Positive Comment:**_____

What Do I Desire To Improve In My Life Today? _____
_____
_____
_____

What Will I Do to Achieve the Imrovement? _____
_____
_____
_____

What Challenges Or Stressors Did I Face Today? _____
_____
_____
_____

What Did Or Will I Do To Rise To The Challenges? _____
_____
_____
_____

What Did I Learn from Today's Experiences? _____
_____
_____
_____

What Am I Grateful for Today? _____
_____
_____
_____

How Did I Improve My Personal Rhythms For...?

*Exercise:*_____

*Nutrition:*_____

Sleep: _____

Date:_____

Date:_____   **Positive Comment:**_____

What Do I Desire To Improve In My Life Today? _____

_____

_____

_____

What Will I Do to Achieve the Imrovement? _____

_____

_____

_____

What Challenges Or Stressors Did I Face Today? _____

_____

_____

_____

What Did Or Will I Do To Rise To The Challenges? _____

_____

_____

_____

What Did I Learn from Today's Experiences? _____

_____

_____

_____

What Am I Grateful for Today? _____

_____

_____

_____

How Did I Improve My Personal Rhythms For…?

*Exercise:*_____

*Nutrition:*_____

Sleep: _____

Date:_____

_____
_____
_____
_____
_____
_____
_____
_____
_____
_____
_____
_____

WEEKLY REVIEW

Areas where I felt successful this week

_____
_____
_____

Areas that I feel I need to focus on this week

_____
_____
_____

Positive personal comment for the week

_____
_____
_____

Most valuable lesson learned this week

_____
_____
_____

Date:_____   **Positive Comment:**_____

What Do I Desire To Improve In My Life Today? _____
_____
_____
_____

What Will I Do to Achieve the Imrovement? _____
_____
_____
_____

What Challenges Or Stressors Did I Face Today? _____
_____
_____
_____

What Did Or Will I Do To Rise To The Challenges? _____
_____
_____
_____

What Did I Learn from Today's Experiences? _____
_____
_____
_____

What Am I Grateful for Today? _____
_____
_____
_____

How Did I Improve My Personal Rhythms For…?

*Exercise:*_____

*Nutrition:*_____

Sleep: _____

Date:_____

_____

_____

_____

_____

_____

_____

_____

_____

_____

_____

_____

_____

_____

_____

_____

_____

_____

_____

_____

_____

_____

_____

_____

_____

_____

_____

_____

_____

_____

_____

_____

Date:_____   **Positive Comment:**_____

What Do I Desire To Improve In My Life Today? _____
_____
_____
_____

What Will I Do to Achieve the Imrovement? _____
_____
_____
_____

What Challenges Or Stressors Did I Face Today? _____
_____
_____
_____

What Did Or Will I Do To Rise To The Challenges? _____
_____
_____
_____

What Did I Learn from Today's Experiences? _____
_____
_____
_____

What Am I Grateful for Today? _____
_____
_____
_____

How Did I Improve My Personal Rhythms For…?

Exercise: _____

*Nutrition:*_____

Sleep: _____

Date:_____

Date:_____ **Positive Comment:**_____

What Do I Desire To Improve In My Life Today? _____

_____

_____

_____

What Will I Do to Achieve the Imrovement? _____

_____

_____

_____

What Challenges Or Stressors Did I Face Today? _____

_____

_____

_____

What Did Or Will I Do To Rise To The Challenges? _____

_____

_____

_____

What Did I Learn from Today's Experiences? _____

_____

_____

_____

What Am I Grateful for Today? _____

_____

_____

_____

How Did I Improve My Personal Rhythms For…?

Exercise: _____

Nutrition: _____

Sleep: _____

Date:_____

Date:_____ **Positive Comment:**_____

What Do I Desire To Improve In My Life Today? _____

_____

_____

_____

What Will I Do to Achieve the Imrovement? _____

_____

_____

_____

What Challenges Or Stressors Did I Face Today? _____

_____

_____

_____

What Did Or Will I Do To Rise To The Challenges? _____

_____

_____

_____

What Did I Learn from Today's Experiences? _____

_____

_____

_____

What Am I Grateful for Today? _____

_____

_____

_____

How Did I Improve My Personal Rhythms For…?

*Exercise:*_____

*Nutrition:*_____

Sleep: _____

Date:_____

Date:_____   **Positive Comment:**_____

What Do I Desire To Improve In My Life Today? _____
_____
_____
_____

What Will I Do to Achieve the Imrovement? _____
_____
_____
_____

What Challenges Or Stressors Did I Face Today? _____
_____
_____
_____

What Did Or Will I Do To Rise To The Challenges? _____
_____
_____
_____

What Did I Learn from Today's Experiences? _____
_____
_____
_____

What Am I Grateful for Today? _____
_____
_____
_____

How Did I Improve My Personal Rhythms For…?

*Exercise:*_____

*Nutrition:*_____

Sleep: _____

Date:_____

_____
_____
_____
_____
_____
_____
_____
_____
_____
_____
_____
_____
_____
_____
_____
_____
_____
_____
_____
_____
_____
_____
_____
_____
_____
_____
_____
_____
_____
_____
_____
_____
_____

Date:_____   **Positive Comment:**_____

What Do I Desire To Improve In My Life Today? _____

_____

_____

_____

What Will I Do to Achieve the Imrovement? _____

_____

_____

_____

What Challenges Or Stressors Did I Face Today? _____

_____

_____

_____

What Did Or Will I Do To Rise To The Challenges? _____

_____

_____

_____

What Did I Learn from Today's Experiences? _____

_____

_____

_____

What Am I Grateful for Today? _____

_____

_____

_____

How Did I Improve My Personal Rhythms For…?

Exercise: _____

Nutrition: _____

Sleep: _____

Date:_____

_____

_____

_____

_____

_____

_____

_____

_____

_____

_____

_____

_____

_____

_____

WEEKLY REVIEW

Areas where I felt successful this week

_____

_____

_____

Areas that I feel I need to focus on this week

_____

_____

_____

Positive personal comment for the week

_____

_____

_____

Most valuable lesson learned this week

_____

_____

_____

Date:_____   **Positive Comment:**_____

What Do I Desire To Improve In My Life Today? _____
_____
_____
_____

What Will I Do to Achieve the Imrovement? _____
_____
_____
_____

What Challenges Or Stressors Did I Face Today? _____
_____
_____
_____

What Did Or Will I Do To Rise To The Challenges? _____
_____
_____
_____

What Did I Learn from Today's Experiences? _____
_____
_____
_____

What Am I Grateful for Today? _____
_____
_____
_____

How Did I Improve My Personal Rhythms For…?

*Exercise:*_____

*Nutrition:*_____

Sleep: _____

Date:_____

Date:_____   **Positive Comment:**_____

What Do I Desire To Improve In My Life Today? _____
_____
_____
_____

What Will I Do to Achieve the Imrovement? _____
_____
_____
_____

What Challenges Or Stressors Did I Face Today? _____
_____
_____
_____

What Did Or Will I Do To Rise To The Challenges? _____
_____
_____
_____

What Did I Learn from Today's Experiences? _____
_____
_____
_____

What Am I Grateful for Today? _____
_____
_____
_____

How Did I Improve My Personal Rhythms For…?

Exercise: _____

Nutrition: _____

Sleep: _____

Date:_____

Date:_____   **Positive Comment:**_____

*What Do I Desire To Improve In My Life Today?*_____
_____
_____
_____

*What Will I Do to Achieve the Imrovement?*_____
_____
_____
_____

*What Challenges Or Stressors Did I Face Today?*_____
_____
_____
_____

*What Did Or Will I Do To Rise To The Challenges?*_____
_____
_____
_____

*What Did I Learn from Today's Experiences?*_____
_____
_____
_____

*What Am I Grateful for Today?*_____
_____
_____
_____

How Did I Improve My Personal Rhythms For…?

*Exercise:*_____

*Nutrition:*_____

*Sleep:*_____

Date:_____

Date:_____   **Positive Comment:**_____

What Do I Desire To Improve In My Life Today? _____
_____
_____
_____

What Will I Do to Achieve the Imrovement? _____
_____
_____
_____

What Challenges Or Stressors Did I Face Today? _____
_____
_____
_____

What Did Or Will I Do To Rise To The Challenges? _____
_____
_____
_____

What Did I Learn from Today's Experiences? _____
_____
_____
_____

What Am I Grateful for Today? _____
_____
_____
_____

How Did I Improve My Personal Rhythms For…?

Exercise: _____

*Nutrition:*_____

Sleep: _____

Date:_____

_____
_____
_____
_____
_____
_____
_____
_____
_____
_____
_____
_____
_____
_____
_____
_____
_____
_____
_____
_____
_____
_____
_____
_____
_____
_____
_____
_____
_____
_____
_____

Date:_____   **Positive Comment:**_____

What Do I Desire To Improve In My Life Today? _____
_____
_____
_____

What Will I Do to Achieve the Imrovement? _____
_____
_____
_____

What Challenges Or Stressors Did I Face Today? _____
_____
_____
_____

What Did Or Will I Do To Rise To The Challenges? _____
_____
_____
_____

What Did I Learn from Today's Experiences? _____
_____
_____
_____

What Am I Grateful for Today? _____
_____
_____
_____

How Did I Improve My Personal Rhythms For…?

*Exercise:*_____

*Nutrition:*_____

Sleep: _____

Date:_____

Date:_____   **Positive Comment:**_____

What Do I Desire To Improve In My Life Today? _____

_____

_____

_____

What Will I Do to Achieve the Imrovement? _____

_____

_____

_____

What Challenges Or Stressors Did I Face Today? _____

_____

_____

_____

What Did Or Will I Do To Rise To The Challenges? _____

_____

_____

_____

What Did I Learn from Today's Experiences? _____

_____

_____

_____

What Am I Grateful for Today? _____

_____

_____

_____

How Did I Improve My Personal Rhythms For…?

Exercise: _____

*Nutrition:*_____

Sleep: _____

Date:_____

_____
_____
_____
_____
_____
_____
_____
_____
_____
_____
_____
_____
_____

WEEKLY REVIEW

Areas where I felt successful this week

_____
_____
_____

Areas that I feel I need to focus on this week

_____
_____
_____

Positive personal comment for the week

_____
_____
_____

Most valuable lesson learned this week

_____
_____
_____

Date:_____   Positive Comment:_____

What Do I Desire To Improve In My Life Today? _____
_____
_____
_____

What Will I Do to Achieve the Imrovement? _____
_____
_____
_____

What Challenges Or Stressors Did I Face Today? _____
_____
_____
_____

What Did Or Will I Do To Rise To The Challenges? _____
_____
_____
_____

What Did I Learn from Today's Experiences? _____
_____
_____
_____

What Am I Grateful for Today? _____
_____
_____
_____

How Did I Improve My Personal Rhythms For…?

Exercise: _____

Nutrition: _____

Sleep: _____

Date:_____

_____
_____
_____
_____
_____
_____
_____
_____
_____
_____
_____
_____
_____
_____
_____
_____
_____
_____
_____
_____
_____
_____
_____
_____
_____
_____
_____
_____
_____
_____

Date:_____   **Positive Comment:**_____

What Do I Desire To Improve In My Life Today? _____

_____

_____

_____

What Will I Do to Achieve the Imrovement? _____

_____

_____

_____

What Challenges Or Stressors Did I Face Today? _____

_____

_____

_____

What Did Or Will I Do To Rise To The Challenges? _____

_____

_____

_____

What Did I Learn from Today's Experiences? _____

_____

_____

_____

What Am I Grateful for Today? _____

_____

_____

_____

How Did I Improve My Personal Rhythms For...?

Exercise: _____

*Nutrition:*_____

Sleep: _____

Date:_____

Date:_____   **Positive Comment:**_____

What Do I Desire To Improve In My Life Today? _____

_____

_____

_____

What Will I Do to Achieve the Imrovement? _____

_____

_____

_____

What Challenges Or Stressors Did I Face Today? _____

_____

_____

_____

What Did Or Will I Do To Rise To The Challenges? _____

_____

_____

_____

What Did I Learn from Today's Experiences? _____

_____

_____

_____

What Am I Grateful for Today? _____

_____

_____

_____

How Did I Improve My Personal Rhythms For…?

*Exercise:*_____

*Nutrition:*_____

Sleep: _____

Date:_____

Date:_____   **Positive Comment:**_____

What Do I Desire To Improve In My Life Today? _____

_____

_____

_____

What Will I Do to Achieve the Imrovement? _____

_____

_____

_____

_____

What Challenges Or Stressors Did I Face Today? _____

_____

_____

_____

What Did Or Will I Do To Rise To The Challenges? _____

_____

_____

_____

What Did I Learn from Today's Experiences? _____

_____

_____

_____

What Am I Grateful for Today? _____

_____

_____

_____

How Did I Improve My Personal Rhythms For...?

*Exercise:*_____

*Nutrition:*_____

Sleep: _____

Date:_____

_____

_____

_____

_____

_____

_____

_____

_____

_____

_____

_____

_____

_____

_____

_____

_____

_____

_____

_____

_____

_____

_____

_____

_____

_____

_____

_____

_____

_____

_____

Date:_____ **Positive Comment:**_____

What Do I Desire To Improve In My Life Today? _____

_____

_____

_____

What Will I Do to Achieve the Imrovement? _____

_____

_____

_____

_____

What Challenges Or Stressors Did I Face Today? _____

_____

_____

_____

What Did Or Will I Do To Rise To The Challenges? _____

_____

_____

_____

What Did I Learn from Today's Experiences? _____

_____

_____

_____

What Am I Grateful for Today? _____

_____

_____

_____

How Did I Improve My Personal Rhythms For…?

*Exercise:*_____

*Nutrition:*_____

Sleep: _____

Date:_____

Date:_____   **Positive Comment:**_____

What Do I Desire To Improve In My Life Today? _____

_____

_____

_____

What Will I Do to Achieve the Imrovement? _____

_____

_____

_____

What Challenges Or Stressors Did I Face Today? _____

_____

_____

_____

What Did Or Will I Do To Rise To The Challenges? _____

_____

_____

_____

What Did I Learn from Today's Experiences? _____

_____

_____

_____

What Am I Grateful for Today? _____

_____

_____

_____

How Did I Improve My Personal Rhythms For…?

Exercise: _____

*Nutrition:*_____

Sleep: _____

Date:_____

_____

_____

_____

_____

_____

_____

_____

_____

_____

_____

_____

_____

WEEKLY REVIEW

Areas where I felt successful this week

_____

_____

_____

Areas that I feel I need to focus on this week

_____

_____

_____

Positive personal comment for the week

_____

_____

_____

Most valuable lesson learned this week

_____

_____

_____

Date:_____ Positive Comment:_____

What Do I Desire To Improve In My Life Today? _____
_____
_____
_____

What Will I Do to Achieve the Imrovement? _____
_____
_____
_____

What Challenges Or Stressors Did I Face Today? _____
_____
_____
_____

What Did Or Will I Do To Rise To The Challenges? _____
_____
_____
_____

What Did I Learn from Today's Experiences? _____
_____
_____
_____

What Am I Grateful for Today? _____
_____
_____
_____

How Did I Improve My Personal Rhythms For…?

Exercise: _____
Nutrition: _____
Sleep: _____

Date:_____

Date:_____ **Positive Comment:**_____

*What Do I Desire To Improve In My Life Today?*_____

_____

_____

_____

*What Will I Do to Achieve the Imrovement?*_____

_____

_____

_____

*What Challenges Or Stressors Did I Face Today?*_____

_____

_____

_____

*What Did Or Will I Do To Rise To The Challenges?*_____

_____

_____

_____

*What Did I Learn from Today's Experiences?*_____

_____

_____

_____

*What Am I Grateful for Today?*_____

_____

_____

_____

How Did I Improve My Personal Rhythms For…?

*Exercise:*_____

*Nutrition:*_____

*Sleep:*_____

Date:_____

Date:_____   **Positive Comment:**_____

What Do I Desire To Improve In My Life Today? _____

_____

_____

_____

What Will I Do to Achieve the Imrovement? _____

_____

_____

_____

What Challenges Or Stressors Did I Face Today? _____

_____

_____

_____

What Did Or Will I Do To Rise To The Challenges? _____

_____

_____

_____

What Did I Learn from Today's Experiences? _____

_____

_____

_____

What Am I Grateful for Today? _____

_____

_____

_____

How Did I Improve My Personal Rhythms For...?

*Exercise:*_____

*Nutrition:*_____

Sleep: _____

Date:_____

Date:_____ **Positive Comment:**_____

What Do I Desire To Improve In My Life Today? _____

_____

_____

_____

What Will I Do to Achieve the Imrovement? _____

_____

_____

_____

What Challenges Or Stressors Did I Face Today? _____

_____

_____

_____

What Did Or Will I Do To Rise To The Challenges? _____

_____

_____

_____

What Did I Learn from Today's Experiences? _____

_____

_____

_____

What Am I Grateful for Today? _____

_____

_____

_____

How Did I Improve My Personal Rhythms For…?

Exercise: _____

Nutrition: _____

Sleep: _____

Date:_____

Date:_____ **Positive Comment:**_____

What Do I Desire To Improve In My Life Today? _____
_____
_____
_____

What Will I Do to Achieve the Imrovement? _____
_____
_____
_____

What Challenges Or Stressors Did I Face Today? _____
_____
_____
_____

What Did Or Will I Do To Rise To The Challenges? _____
_____
_____
_____

What Did I Learn from Today's Experiences? _____
_____
_____
_____

What Am I Grateful for Today? _____
_____
_____
_____

How Did I Improve My Personal Rhythms For…?

*Exercise:*_____

*Nutrition:*_____

Sleep: _____

Date:_____

Date:_____   **Positive Comment:**_____

What Do I Desire To Improve In My Life Today? _____
_____
_____
_____

What Will I Do to Achieve the Imrovement? _____
_____
_____
_____

What Challenges Or Stressors Did I Face Today? _____
_____
_____
_____

What Did Or Will I Do To Rise To The Challenges? _____
_____
_____
_____

What Did I Learn from Today's Experiences? _____
_____
_____
_____

What Am I Grateful for Today? _____
_____
_____
_____

How Did I Improve My Personal Rhythms For…?

Exercise: _____

*Nutrition:*_____

Sleep: _____

Date:_____

_____
_____
_____
_____
_____
_____
_____
_____
_____
_____
_____
_____

WEEKLY REVIEW

Areas where I felt successful this week

_____
_____
_____

Areas that I feel I need to focus on this week

_____
_____
_____

Positive personal comment for the week

_____
_____
_____

Most valuable lesson learned this week

_____
_____
_____

Date: _____   **Positive Comment:** _____

What Do I Desire To Improve In My Life Today? _____

_____

_____

_____

What Will I Do to Achieve the Imrovement? _____

_____

_____

_____

What Challenges Or Stressors Did I Face Today? _____

_____

_____

_____

What Did Or Will I Do To Rise To The Challenges? _____

_____

_____

_____

What Did I Learn from Today's Experiences? _____

_____

_____

_____

What Am I Grateful for Today? _____

_____

_____

_____

How Did I Improve My Personal Rhythms For…?

Exercise: _____

Nutrition: _____

Sleep: _____

Date:_____

_____
_____
_____
_____
_____
_____
_____
_____
_____
_____
_____
_____
_____
_____
_____
_____
_____
_____
_____
_____
_____
_____
_____
_____
_____
_____
_____
_____
_____

Date:_____   **Positive Comment:**_____

What Do I Desire To Improve In My Life Today? _____
_____
_____
_____

What Will I Do to Achieve the Imrovement? _____
_____
_____
_____

What Challenges Or Stressors Did I Face Today? _____
_____
_____
_____

What Did Or Will I Do To Rise To The Challenges? _____
_____
_____
_____

What Did I Learn from Today's Experiences? _____
_____
_____
_____

What Am I Grateful for Today? _____
_____
_____
_____

How Did I Improve My Personal Rhythms For…?

*Exercise:*_____
*Nutrition:*_____
Sleep: _____

Date:_____

Date:_____   **Positive Comment:**_____

What Do I Desire To Improve In My Life Today? _____

_____

_____

_____

What Will I Do to Achieve the Imrovement? _____

_____

_____

_____

What Challenges Or Stressors Did I Face Today? _____

_____

_____

_____

What Did Or Will I Do To Rise To The Challenges? _____

_____

_____

_____

What Did I Learn from Today's Experiences? _____

_____

_____

_____

What Am I Grateful for Today? _____

_____

_____

_____

How Did I Improve My Personal Rhythms For…?

*Exercise:*_____

*Nutrition:*_____

Sleep: _____

Date:_____

Date:_____ **Positive Comment:**_____

What Do I Desire To Improve In My Life Today? _____
_____
_____
_____

What Will I Do to Achieve the Imrovement? _____
_____
_____
_____

What Challenges Or Stressors Did I Face Today? _____
_____
_____
_____

What Did Or Will I Do To Rise To The Challenges? _____
_____
_____
_____

What Did I Learn from Today's Experiences? _____
_____
_____
_____

What Am I Grateful for Today? _____
_____
_____
_____

How Did I Improve My Personal Rhythms For…?

Exercise: _____

Nutrition: _____

Sleep: _____

Date:_____

_____
_____
_____
_____
_____
_____
_____
_____
_____
_____
_____
_____
_____
_____
_____
_____
_____
_____
_____
_____
_____
_____
_____
_____
_____
_____
_____
_____
_____
_____

Date:_____   **Positive Comment:**_____

What Do I Desire To Improve In My Life Today? _____
_____
_____
_____

What Will I Do to Achieve the Imrovement? _____
_____
_____
_____

What Challenges Or Stressors Did I Face Today? _____
_____
_____
_____

What Did Or Will I Do To Rise To The Challenges? _____
_____
_____
_____

What Did I Learn from Today's Experiences? _____
_____
_____
_____

What Am I Grateful for Today? _____
_____
_____
_____

How Did I Improve My Personal Rhythms For…?

*Exercise:*_____

*Nutrition:*_____

Sleep: _____

Date:_____

Date:_____   **Positive Comment:**_____

What Do I Desire To Improve In My Life Today? _____

_____

_____

_____

What Will I Do to Achieve the Imrovement? _____

_____

_____

_____

What Challenges Or Stressors Did I Face Today? _____

_____

_____

_____

What Did Or Will I Do To Rise To The Challenges? _____

_____

_____

_____

What Did I Learn from Today's Experiences? _____

_____

_____

_____

What Am I Grateful for Today? _____

_____

_____

_____

How Did I Improve My Personal Rhythms For…?

Exercise: _____

Nutrition: _____

Sleep: _____

Date:_____

_____

_____

_____

_____

_____

_____

_____

_____

_____

_____

_____

_____

_____

_____

WEEKLY REVIEW

Areas where I felt successful this week

_____

_____

_____

Areas that I feel I need to focus on this week

_____

_____

_____

Positive personal comment for the week

_____

_____

_____

Most valuable lesson learned this week

_____

_____

_____

Date:_____   **Positive Comment:**_____

What Do I Desire To Improve In My Life Today? _____

_____

_____

_____

What Will I Do to Achieve the Imrovement? _____

_____

_____

_____

What Challenges Or Stressors Did I Face Today? _____

_____

_____

_____

What Did Or Will I Do To Rise To The Challenges? _____

_____

_____

_____

What Did I Learn from Today's Experiences? _____

_____

_____

_____

What Am I Grateful for Today? _____

_____

_____

_____

How Did I Improve My Personal Rhythms For…?

Exercise: _____

Nutrition: _____

Sleep: _____

Date:_____

Date:_____   **Positive Comment:**_____

What Do I Desire To Improve In My Life Today? _____

_____

_____

_____

What Will I Do to Achieve the Imrovement? _____

_____

_____

_____

What Challenges Or Stressors Did I Face Today? _____

_____

_____

_____

What Did Or Will I Do To Rise To The Challenges? _____

_____

_____

_____

What Did I Learn from Today's Experiences? _____

_____

_____

_____

What Am I Grateful for Today? _____

_____

_____

_____

How Did I Improve My Personal Rhythms For…?

*Exercise:*_____

*Nutrition:*_____

Sleep: _____

Date:_____

Date:_____   **Positive Comment:**_____

What Do I Desire To Improve In My Life Today? _____
_____
_____
_____

What Will I Do to Achieve the Imrovement? _____
_____
_____
_____

What Challenges Or Stressors Did I Face Today? _____
_____
_____
_____

What Did Or Will I Do To Rise To The Challenges? _____
_____
_____
_____

What Did I Learn from Today's Experiences? _____
_____
_____
_____

What Am I Grateful for Today? _____
_____
_____
_____

How Did I Improve My Personal Rhythms For…?

*Exercise:*_____
*Nutrition:*_____
Sleep: _____

Date:_____

Date:_____   **Positive Comment:**_____

What Do I Desire To Improve In My Life Today? _____

_____

_____

_____

What Will I Do to Achieve the Imrovement? _____

_____

_____

_____

What Challenges Or Stressors Did I Face Today? _____

_____

_____

_____

What Did Or Will I Do To Rise To The Challenges? _____

_____

_____

_____

What Did I Learn from Today's Experiences? _____

_____

_____

_____

What Am I Grateful for Today? _____

_____

_____

_____

How Did I Improve My Personal Rhythms For…?

Exercise: _____

*Nutrition:*_____

Sleep: _____

Date:_____

Date:_____   **Positive Comment:**_____

What Do I Desire To Improve In My Life Today? _____
_____
_____
_____

What Will I Do to Achieve the Imrovement? _____
_____
_____
_____

What Challenges Or Stressors Did I Face Today? _____
_____
_____
_____

What Did Or Will I Do To Rise To The Challenges? _____
_____
_____
_____

What Did I Learn from Today's Experiences? _____
_____
_____
_____

What Am I Grateful for Today? _____
_____
_____
_____

How Did I Improve My Personal Rhythms For…?

Exercise: _____

Nutrition: _____

Sleep: _____

Date:_____

Date:_____   **Positive Comment:**_____

*What Do I Desire To Improve In My Life Today?*_____

_____

_____

_____

*What Will I Do to Achieve the Imrovement?*_____

_____

_____

_____

_____

*What Challenges Or Stressors Did I Face Today?*_____

_____

_____

_____

*What Did Or Will I Do To Rise To The Challenges?*_____

_____

_____

_____

*What Did I Learn from Today's Experiences?*_____

_____

_____

_____

*What Am I Grateful for Today?*_____

_____

_____

_____

How Did I Improve My Personal Rhythms For…?

*Exercise:*_____

*Nutrition:*_____

*Sleep:*_____

Date:_____

_____

_____

_____

_____

_____

_____

_____

_____

_____

_____

_____

_____

WEEKLY REVIEW

Areas where I felt successful this week

_____

_____

_____

Areas that I feel I need to focus on this week

_____

_____

_____

Positive personal comment for the week

_____

_____

_____

Most valuable lesson learned this week

_____

_____

_____

Date:_____   **Positive Comment:**_____

What Do I Desire To Improve In My Life Today? _____
_____
_____
_____

What Will I Do to Achieve the Imrovement? _____
_____
_____
_____

What Challenges Or Stressors Did I Face Today? _____
_____
_____
_____

What Did Or Will I Do To Rise To The Challenges? _____
_____
_____
_____

What Did I Learn from Today's Experiences? _____
_____
_____
_____

What Am I Grateful for Today? _____
_____
_____
_____

How Did I Improve My Personal Rhythms For...?

Exercise: _____

*Nutrition:*_____

Sleep: _____

Date:_____

Date:_____   **Positive Comment:**_____

What Do I Desire To Improve In My Life Today? _____

_____

_____

_____

What Will I Do to Achieve the Imrovement? _____

_____

_____

_____

What Challenges Or Stressors Did I Face Today? _____

_____

_____

_____

What Did Or Will I Do To Rise To The Challenges? _____

_____

_____

_____

What Did I Learn from Today's Experiences? _____

_____

_____

_____

What Am I Grateful for Today? _____

_____

_____

_____

How Did I Improve My Personal Rhythms For…?

*Exercise:*_____

*Nutrition:*_____

Sleep: _____

Date:_____

Date:_____   **Positive Comment:**_____

What Do I Desire To Improve In My Life Today? _____

_____

_____

_____

What Will I Do to Achieve the Imrovement? _____

_____

_____

_____

What Challenges Or Stressors Did I Face Today? _____

_____

_____

_____

What Did Or Will I Do To Rise To The Challenges? _____

_____

_____

_____

What Did I Learn from Today's Experiences? _____

_____

_____

_____

What Am I Grateful for Today? _____

_____

_____

_____

How Did I Improve My Personal Rhythms For…?

*Exercise:*_____

*Nutrition:*_____

Sleep: _____

Date:_____

Date:_____   **Positive Comment:**_____

What Do I Desire To Improve In My Life Today? _____
_____
_____
_____

What Will I Do to Achieve the Imrovement? _____
_____
_____
_____

What Challenges Or Stressors Did I Face Today? _____
_____
_____
_____

What Did Or Will I Do To Rise To The Challenges? _____
_____
_____
_____

What Did I Learn from Today's Experiences? _____
_____
_____
_____

What Am I Grateful for Today? _____
_____
_____
_____

How Did I Improve My Personal Rhythms For…?

Exercise: _____

*Nutrition:*_____

Sleep: _____

Date:_____

Date:_____   **Positive Comment:**_____

What Do I Desire To Improve In My Life Today? _____
_____
_____
_____

What Will I Do to Achieve the Imrovement? _____
_____
_____
_____

What Challenges Or Stressors Did I Face Today? _____
_____
_____
_____

What Did Or Will I Do To Rise To The Challenges? _____
_____
_____
_____

What Did I Learn from Today's Experiences? _____
_____
_____
_____

What Am I Grateful for Today? _____
_____
_____
_____

How Did I Improve My Personal Rhythms For…?

*Exercise:*_____

*Nutrition:*_____

Sleep: _____

Date:_____

Date:_____   **Positive Comment:**_____

What Do I Desire To Improve In My Life Today? _____

_____

_____

_____

What Will I Do to Achieve the Imrovement? _____

_____

_____

_____

What Challenges Or Stressors Did I Face Today? _____

_____

_____

_____

What Did Or Will I Do To Rise To The Challenges? _____

_____

_____

_____

What Did I Learn from Today's Experiences? _____

_____

_____

_____

What Am I Grateful for Today? _____

_____

_____

_____

How Did I Improve My Personal Rhythms For…?

*Exercise:*_____

*Nutrition:*_____

Sleep: _____

Date:_____

_____

_____

_____

_____

_____

_____

_____

_____

_____

_____

_____

_____

_____

WEEKLY REVIEW

Areas where I felt successful this week

_____

_____

_____

Areas that I feel I need to focus on this week

_____

_____

_____

Positive personal comment for the week

_____

_____

_____

Most valuable lesson learned this week

_____

_____

_____

Date:_____   Positive Comment:_____

What Do I Desire To Improve In My Life Today? _____
_____
_____
_____

What Will I Do to Achieve the Imrovement? _____
_____
_____
_____

What Challenges Or Stressors Did I Face Today? _____
_____
_____
_____

What Did Or Will I Do To Rise To The Challenges? _____
_____
_____
_____

What Did I Learn from Today's Experiences? _____
_____
_____
_____

What Am I Grateful for Today? _____
_____
_____
_____

How Did I Improve My Personal Rhythms For…?

Exercise: _____

Nutrition: _____

Sleep: _____

Date:_____

Date:_____   **Positive Comment:**_____

What Do I Desire To Improve In My Life Today? _____

_____

_____

_____

What Will I Do to Achieve the Imrovement? _____

_____

_____

_____

What Challenges Or Stressors Did I Face Today? _____

_____

_____

_____

What Did Or Will I Do To Rise To The Challenges? _____

_____

_____

_____

What Did I Learn from Today's Experiences? _____

_____

_____

_____

What Am I Grateful for Today? _____

_____

_____

_____

How Did I Improve My Personal Rhythms For…?

*Exercise:*_____

*Nutrition:*_____

Sleep: _____

Date:_____

Date:_____   **Positive Comment:**_____

What Do I Desire To Improve In My Life Today? _____

_____

_____

_____

What Will I Do to Achieve the Imrovement? _____

_____

_____

_____

What Challenges Or Stressors Did I Face Today? _____

_____

_____

_____

What Did Or Will I Do To Rise To The Challenges? _____

_____

_____

_____

What Did I Learn from Today's Experiences? _____

_____

_____

_____

What Am I Grateful for Today? _____

_____

_____

_____

How Did I Improve My Personal Rhythms For…?

*Exercise:*_____

*Nutrition:*_____

Sleep: _____

Date:_____

Date:_____   **Positive Comment:**_____

What Do I Desire To Improve In My Life Today? _____
_____
_____
_____

What Will I Do to Achieve the Imrovement? _____
_____
_____
_____

What Challenges Or Stressors Did I Face Today? _____
_____
_____
_____

What Did Or Will I Do To Rise To The Challenges? _____
_____
_____
_____

What Did I Learn from Today's Experiences? _____
_____
_____
_____

What Am I Grateful for Today? _____
_____
_____
_____

How Did I Improve My Personal Rhythms For…?
*Exercise:*_____
*Nutrition:*_____
Sleep: _____

Date:_____

Date:_____   **Positive Comment:**_____

What Do I Desire To Improve In My Life Today? _____
_____
_____
_____

What Will I Do to Achieve the Imrovement? _____
_____
_____
_____

What Challenges Or Stressors Did I Face Today? _____
_____
_____
_____

What Did Or Will I Do To Rise To The Challenges? _____
_____
_____
_____

What Did I Learn from Today's Experiences? _____
_____
_____
_____

What Am I Grateful for Today? _____
_____
_____
_____

How Did I Improve My Personal Rhythms For...?

*Exercise:*_____

*Nutrition:*_____

Sleep: _____

Date:_____

Date:_____ **Positive Comment:**_____

What Do I Desire To Improve In My Life Today? _____

_____

_____

_____

What Will I Do to Achieve the Imrovement? _____

_____

_____

_____

What Challenges Or Stressors Did I Face Today? _____

_____

_____

_____

What Did Or Will I Do To Rise To The Challenges? _____

_____

_____

_____

What Did I Learn from Today's Experiences? _____

_____

_____

_____

What Am I Grateful for Today? _____

_____

_____

_____

How Did I Improve My Personal Rhythms For…?

Exercise: _____

*Nutrition:*_____

Sleep: _____

Date:_____

_____

_____

_____

_____

_____

_____

_____

_____

_____

_____

_____

WEEKLY REVIEW

Areas where I felt successful this week

_____

_____

_____

Areas that I feel I need to focus on this week

_____

_____

_____

Positive personal comment for the week

_____

_____

_____

Most valuable lesson learned this week

_____

_____

_____

Date:_____   **Positive Comment:**_____

What Do I Desire To Improve In My Life Today? _____
_____
_____
_____

What Will I Do to Achieve the Imrovement? _____
_____
_____
_____

What Challenges Or Stressors Did I Face Today? _____
_____
_____
_____

What Did Or Will I Do To Rise To The Challenges? _____
_____
_____
_____

What Did I Learn from Today's Experiences? _____
_____
_____
_____

What Am I Grateful for Today? _____
_____
_____
_____

How Did I Improve My Personal Rhythms For…?

*Exercise:*_____

*Nutrition:*_____

Sleep: _____

Date:_____

_____
_____
_____
_____
_____
_____
_____
_____
_____
_____
_____
_____
_____
_____
_____
_____
_____
_____
_____
_____
_____
_____
_____
_____
_____
_____
_____
_____
_____

Date:_____   **Positive Comment:**_____

What Do I Desire To Improve In My Life Today? _____
_____
_____
_____

What Will I Do to Achieve the Imrovement? _____
_____
_____
_____

What Challenges Or Stressors Did I Face Today? _____
_____
_____
_____

What Did Or Will I Do To Rise To The Challenges? _____
_____
_____
_____

What Did I Learn from Today's Experiences? _____
_____
_____
_____

What Am I Grateful for Today? _____
_____
_____
_____

How Did I Improve My Personal Rhythms For…?

*Exercise:*_____

*Nutrition:*_____

Sleep: _____

Date:_____

Date:_____   **Positive Comment:**_____

What Do I Desire To Improve In My Life Today? _____

_____

_____

_____

What Will I Do to Achieve the Imrovement? _____

_____

_____

_____

What Challenges Or Stressors Did I Face Today? _____

_____

_____

_____

What Did Or Will I Do To Rise To The Challenges? _____

_____

_____

_____

What Did I Learn from Today's Experiences? _____

_____

_____

_____

What Am I Grateful for Today? _____

_____

_____

_____

How Did I Improve My Personal Rhythms For…?

Exercise: _____

Nutrition: _____

Sleep: _____

Date:_____

Date:_____   **Positive Comment:**_____

What Do I Desire To Improve In My Life Today? _____

_____

_____

_____

What Will I Do to Achieve the Imrovement? _____

_____

_____

_____

What Challenges Or Stressors Did I Face Today? _____

_____

_____

_____

What Did Or Will I Do To Rise To The Challenges? _____

_____

_____

_____

What Did I Learn from Today's Experiences? _____

_____

_____

_____

What Am I Grateful for Today? _____

_____

_____

_____

How Did I Improve My Personal Rhythms For…?

Exercise: _____

*Nutrition:*_____

Sleep: _____

Date:_____

Date:_____   **Positive Comment:**_____

What Do I Desire To Improve In My Life Today? _____
_____
_____
_____

What Will I Do to Achieve the Imrovement? _____
_____
_____
_____

What Challenges Or Stressors Did I Face Today? _____
_____
_____
_____

What Did Or Will I Do To Rise To The Challenges? _____
_____
_____
_____

What Did I Learn from Today's Experiences? _____
_____
_____
_____

What Am I Grateful for Today? _____
_____
_____
_____

How Did I Improve My Personal Rhythms For…?

Exercise: _____

*Nutrition:*_____

Sleep: _____

Date:_____

_____

_____

_____

_____

_____

_____

_____

_____

_____

_____

_____

_____

_____

_____

_____

_____

_____

_____

_____

_____

_____

_____

_____

_____

_____

_____

_____

_____

_____

_____

Date:_____ **Positive Comment:**_____

What Do I Desire To Improve In My Life Today? _____

_____

_____

_____

What Will I Do to Achieve the Imrovement? _____

_____

_____

_____

What Challenges Or Stressors Did I Face Today? _____

_____

_____

_____

What Did Or Will I Do To Rise To The Challenges? _____

_____

_____

_____

What Did I Learn from Today's Experiences? _____

_____

_____

_____

What Am I Grateful for Today? _____

_____

_____

_____

How Did I Improve My Personal Rhythms For…?

*Exercise:*_____

*Nutrition:*_____

Sleep: _____

Date:_____

_____

_____

_____

_____

_____

_____

_____

_____

_____

_____

_____

_____

_____

_____

WEEKLY REVIEW

Areas where I felt successful this week

_____

_____

_____

Areas that I feel I need to focus on this week

_____

_____

_____

Positive personal comment for the week

_____

_____

_____

Most valuable lesson learned this week

_____

_____

_____

Date:_____ **Positive Comment:**_____

What Do I Desire To Improve In My Life Today? _____

_____

_____

_____

What Will I Do to Achieve the Imrovement? _____

_____

_____

_____

What Challenges Or Stressors Did I Face Today? _____

_____

_____

_____

What Did Or Will I Do To Rise To The Challenges? _____

_____

_____

_____

What Did I Learn from Today's Experiences? _____

_____

_____

_____

What Am I Grateful for Today? _____

_____

_____

_____

How Did I Improve My Personal Rhythms For…?

*Exercise:*_____

*Nutrition:*_____

Sleep: _____

Date:_____

_____
_____
_____
_____
_____
_____
_____
_____
_____
_____
_____
_____
_____
_____
_____
_____
_____
_____
_____
_____
_____
_____
_____
_____
_____
_____
_____
_____
_____
_____
_____
_____

Date:_____   **Positive Comment:**_____

What Do I Desire To Improve In My Life Today? _____

_____

_____

_____

What Will I Do to Achieve the Imrovement? _____

_____

_____

_____

What Challenges Or Stressors Did I Face Today? _____

_____

_____

_____

What Did Or Will I Do To Rise To The Challenges? _____

_____

_____

_____

What Did I Learn from Today's Experiences? _____

_____

_____

_____

What Am I Grateful for Today? _____

_____

_____

_____

How Did I Improve My Personal Rhythms For…?

Exercise: _____

*Nutrition:*_____

Sleep: _____

Date:_____

Date:_____ **Positive Comment:**_____

What Do I Desire To Improve In My Life Today? _____
_____
_____
_____

What Will I Do to Achieve the Imrovement? _____
_____
_____
_____

What Challenges Or Stressors Did I Face Today? _____
_____
_____
_____

What Did Or Will I Do To Rise To The Challenges? _____
_____
_____
_____

What Did I Learn from Today's Experiences? _____
_____
_____
_____

What Am I Grateful for Today? _____
_____
_____
_____

How Did I Improve My Personal Rhythms For...?

*Exercise:*_____

*Nutrition:*_____

Sleep: _____

Date:_____

Date:_____   **Positive Comment:**_____

*What Do I Desire To Improve In My Life Today?*_____

_____

_____

_____

*What Will I Do to Achieve the Imrovement?*_____

_____

_____

_____

*What Challenges Or Stressors Did I Face Today?*_____

_____

_____

_____

*What Did Or Will I Do To Rise To The Challenges?*_____

_____

_____

_____

*What Did I Learn from Today's Experiences?*_____

_____

_____

_____

*What Am I Grateful for Today?*_____

_____

_____

_____

How Did I Improve My Personal Rhythms For…?

*Exercise:*_____

*Nutrition:*_____

*Sleep:*_____

Date:_____

_____
_____
_____
_____
_____
_____
_____
_____
_____
_____
_____
_____
_____
_____
_____
_____
_____
_____
_____
_____
_____
_____
_____
_____
_____
_____
_____
_____
_____
_____
_____
_____

Date:_____ **Positive Comment:**_____

What Do I Desire To Improve In My Life Today? _____

_____

_____

_____

What Will I Do to Achieve the Imrovement? _____

_____

_____

_____

What Challenges Or Stressors Did I Face Today? _____

_____

_____

_____

What Did Or Will I Do To Rise To The Challenges? _____

_____

_____

_____

What Did I Learn from Today's Experiences? _____

_____

_____

_____

What Am I Grateful for Today? _____

_____

_____

_____

How Did I Improve My Personal Rhythms For…?

*Exercise:*_____

*Nutrition:*_____

Sleep: _____

Date:_____

Date:_____   **Positive Comment:**_____

What Do I Desire To Improve In My Life Today? _____

_____

_____

_____

What Will I Do to Achieve the Imrovement? _____

_____

_____

_____

What Challenges Or Stressors Did I Face Today? _____

_____

_____

_____

What Did Or Will I Do To Rise To The Challenges? _____

_____

_____

_____

What Did I Learn from Today's Experiences? _____

_____

_____

_____

What Am I Grateful for Today? _____

_____

_____

_____

How Did I Improve My Personal Rhythms For…?

Exercise: _____

Nutrition: _____

Sleep: _____

Date:_____

_____

_____

_____

_____

_____

_____

_____

_____

_____

_____

_____

_____

_____

WEEKLY REVIEW

Areas where I felt successful this week

_____

_____

_____

Areas that I feel I need to focus on this week

_____

_____

_____

Positive personal comment for the week

_____

_____

_____

Most valuable lesson learned this week

_____

_____

_____

Date:_____ **Positive Comment:**_____

What Do I Desire To Improve In My Life Today? _____
_____
_____
_____

What Will I Do to Achieve the Imrovement? _____
_____
_____
_____

What Challenges Or Stressors Did I Face Today? _____
_____
_____
_____

What Did Or Will I Do To Rise To The Challenges? _____
_____
_____
_____

What Did I Learn from Today's Experiences? _____
_____
_____
_____

What Am I Grateful for Today? _____
_____
_____
_____

How Did I Improve My Personal Rhythms For…?

*Exercise:*_____

*Nutrition:*_____

Sleep: _____

Date:_____

Date:_____   **Positive Comment:**_____

What Do I Desire To Improve In My Life Today? _____

_____

_____

_____

What Will I Do to Achieve the Imrovement? _____

_____

_____

_____

What Challenges Or Stressors Did I Face Today? _____

_____

_____

_____

What Did Or Will I Do To Rise To The Challenges? _____

_____

_____

_____

What Did I Learn from Today's Experiences? _____

_____

_____

_____

What Am I Grateful for Today? _____

_____

_____

_____

How Did I Improve My Personal Rhythms For…?

*Exercise:*_____

*Nutrition:*_____

Sleep: _____

Date:_____

Date:_____   **Positive Comment:**_____

What Do I Desire To Improve In My Life Today? _____
_____
_____
_____

What Will I Do to Achieve the Imrovement? _____
_____
_____
_____

What Challenges Or Stressors Did I Face Today? _____
_____
_____
_____

What Did Or Will I Do To Rise To The Challenges? _____
_____
_____
_____

What Did I Learn from Today's Experiences? _____
_____
_____
_____

What Am I Grateful for Today? _____
_____
_____
_____

How Did I Improve My Personal Rhythms For...?

Exercise: _____
Nutrition: _____
Sleep: _____

Date:_____

Date:_____ **Positive Comment:**_____

What Do I Desire To Improve In My Life Today? _____
_____
_____
_____

What Will I Do to Achieve the Imrovement? _____
_____
_____
_____

What Challenges Or Stressors Did I Face Today? _____
_____
_____
_____

What Did Or Will I Do To Rise To The Challenges? _____
_____
_____
_____

What Did I Learn from Today's Experiences? _____
_____
_____
_____

What Am I Grateful for Today? _____
_____
_____
_____

How Did I Improve My Personal Rhythms For…?

Exercise: _____
Nutrition: _____
Sleep: _____

Date:_____

Date:_____   **Positive Comment:**_____

What Do I Desire To Improve In My Life Today? _____

_____

_____

_____

What Will I Do to Achieve the Imrovement? _____

_____

_____

_____

What Challenges Or Stressors Did I Face Today? _____

_____

_____

_____

What Did Or Will I Do To Rise To The Challenges? _____

_____

_____

_____

What Did I Learn from Today's Experiences? _____

_____

_____

_____

What Am I Grateful for Today? _____

_____

_____

_____

How Did I Improve My Personal Rhythms For…?

*Exercise:*_____

*Nutrition:*_____

Sleep: _____

Date:_____

Date:_____ **Positive Comment:**_____

What Do I Desire To Improve In My Life Today? _____

_____

_____

_____

What Will I Do to Achieve the Imrovement? _____

_____

_____

_____

What Challenges Or Stressors Did I Face Today? _____

_____

_____

_____

What Did Or Will I Do To Rise To The Challenges? _____

_____

_____

_____

What Did I Learn from Today's Experiences? _____

_____

_____

_____

What Am I Grateful for Today? _____

_____

_____

_____

How Did I Improve My Personal Rhythms For…?

Exercise: _____

Nutrition: _____

Sleep: _____

Date:_____

_____
_____
_____
_____
_____
_____
_____
_____
_____
_____
_____
_____
_____

WEEKLY REVIEW

Areas where I felt successful this week

_____
_____
_____

Areas that I feel I need to focus on this week

_____
_____
_____

Positive personal comment for the week

_____
_____
_____

Most valuable lesson learned this week

_____
_____
_____

Date:_____   **Positive Comment:**_____

What Do I Desire To Improve In My Life Today? _____
_____
_____
_____

What Will I Do to Achieve the Imrovement? _____
_____
_____
_____

What Challenges Or Stressors Did I Face Today? _____
_____
_____
_____

What Did Or Will I Do To Rise To The Challenges? _____
_____
_____
_____

What Did I Learn from Today's Experiences? _____
_____
_____
_____

What Am I Grateful for Today? _____
_____
_____
_____

How Did I Improve My Personal Rhythms For…?

*Exercise:*_____

*Nutrition:*_____

Sleep: _____

Date:_____

Date:_____   **Positive Comment:**_____

What Do I Desire To Improve In My Life Today? _____

_____

_____

_____

What Will I Do to Achieve the Imrovement? _____

_____

_____

_____

What Challenges Or Stressors Did I Face Today? _____

_____

_____

_____

What Did Or Will I Do To Rise To The Challenges? _____

_____

_____

_____

What Did I Learn from Today's Experiences? _____

_____

_____

_____

What Am I Grateful for Today? _____

_____

_____

_____

How Did I Improve My Personal Rhythms For…?

*Exercise:*_____

*Nutrition:*_____

Sleep: _____

Date:_____

Date:_____   **Positive Comment:**_____

What Do I Desire To Improve In My Life Today? _____
_____
_____
_____

What Will I Do to Achieve the Imrovement? _____
_____
_____
_____

What Challenges Or Stressors Did I Face Today? _____
_____
_____
_____

What Did Or Will I Do To Rise To The Challenges? _____
_____
_____
_____

What Did I Learn from Today's Experiences? _____
_____
_____
_____

What Am I Grateful for Today? _____
_____
_____
_____

How Did I Improve My Personal Rhythms For…?

Exercise: _____

*Nutrition:*_____

Sleep: _____

Date:_____

Date:_____   **Positive Comment:**_____

What Do I Desire To Improve In My Life Today? _____

_____

_____

_____

What Will I Do to Achieve the Imrovement? _____

_____

_____

_____

What Challenges Or Stressors Did I Face Today? _____

_____

_____

_____

What Did Or Will I Do To Rise To The Challenges? _____

_____

_____

_____

What Did I Learn from Today's Experiences? _____

_____

_____

_____

What Am I Grateful for Today? _____

_____

_____

_____

How Did I Improve My Personal Rhythms For…?

Exercise: _____

*Nutrition:*_____

Sleep: _____

Date:_____

Date:_____   **Positive Comment:**_____

What Do I Desire To Improve In My Life Today? _____
_____
_____
_____

What Will I Do to Achieve the Imrovement? _____
_____
_____
_____

What Challenges Or Stressors Did I Face Today? _____
_____
_____
_____

What Did Or Will I Do To Rise To The Challenges? _____
_____
_____
_____

What Did I Learn from Today's Experiences? _____
_____
_____
_____

What Am I Grateful for Today? _____
_____
_____
_____

How Did I Improve My Personal Rhythms For...?

*Exercise:*_____

*Nutrition:*_____

Sleep: _____

Date:_____

Date:_____   **Positive Comment:**_____

What Do I Desire To Improve In My Life Today? _____
_____
_____
_____

What Will I Do to Achieve the Imrovement? _____
_____
_____
_____

What Challenges Or Stressors Did I Face Today? _____
_____
_____
_____

What Did Or Will I Do To Rise To The Challenges? _____
_____
_____
_____

What Did I Learn from Today's Experiences? _____
_____
_____
_____

What Am I Grateful for Today? _____
_____
_____
_____

How Did I Improve My Personal Rhythms For...?

Exercise: _____

Nutrition: _____

Sleep: _____

Date:_____

_____
_____
_____
_____
_____
_____
_____
_____
_____
_____
_____
_____

WEEKLY REVIEW

Areas where I felt successful this week

_____
_____
_____

Areas that I feel I need to focus on this week

_____
_____
_____

Positive personal comment for the week

_____
_____
_____

Most valuable lesson learned this week

_____
_____
_____

Date:_____   **Positive Comment:**_____

What Do I Desire To Improve In My Life Today? _____
_____
_____
_____

What Will I Do to Achieve the Imrovement? _____
_____
_____
_____

What Challenges Or Stressors Did I Face Today? _____
_____
_____
_____

What Did Or Will I Do To Rise To The Challenges? _____
_____
_____
_____

What Did I Learn from Today's Experiences? _____
_____
_____
_____

What Am I Grateful for Today? _____
_____
_____
_____

How Did I Improve My Personal Rhythms For…?

Exercise: _____
*Nutrition:*_____
Sleep: _____

Date:_____

Date:_____ **Positive Comment:**_____

What Do I Desire To Improve In My Life Today? _____

_____

_____

_____

What Will I Do to Achieve the Imrovement? _____

_____

_____

_____

_____

What Challenges Or Stressors Did I Face Today? _____

_____

_____

_____

What Did Or Will I Do To Rise To The Challenges? _____

_____

_____

_____

What Did I Learn from Today's Experiences? _____

_____

_____

_____

What Am I Grateful for Today? _____

_____

_____

_____

How Did I Improve My Personal Rhythms For…?

Exercise: _____

Nutrition: _____

Sleep: _____

Date:_____

_____

_____

_____

_____

_____

_____

_____

_____

_____

_____

_____

_____

_____

_____

_____

_____

_____

_____

_____

_____

_____

_____

_____

_____

_____

_____

_____

_____

_____

_____

_____

_____

_____

_____

_____

_____

Date:_____   **Positive Comment:**_____

What Do I Desire To Improve In My Life Today? _____
_____
_____
_____

What Will I Do to Achieve the Imrovement? _____
_____
_____
_____

What Challenges Or Stressors Did I Face Today? _____
_____
_____
_____

What Did Or Will I Do To Rise To The Challenges? _____
_____
_____
_____

What Did I Learn from Today's Experiences? _____
_____
_____
_____

What Am I Grateful for Today? _____
_____
_____
_____

How Did I Improve My Personal Rhythms For...?

*Exercise:*_____

*Nutrition:*_____

Sleep: _____

Date:_____

_____
_____
_____
_____
_____
_____
_____
_____
_____
_____
_____
_____
_____
_____
_____
_____
_____
_____
_____
_____
_____
_____
_____
_____
_____
_____
_____
_____
_____
_____
_____
_____
_____
_____
_____
_____

Date:_____   **Positive Comment:**_____

What Do I Desire To Improve In My Life Today? _____

_____

_____

_____

What Will I Do to Achieve the Imrovement? _____

_____

_____

_____

What Challenges Or Stressors Did I Face Today? _____

_____

_____

_____

What Did Or Will I Do To Rise To The Challenges? _____

_____

_____

_____

What Did I Learn from Today's Experiences? _____

_____

_____

_____

What Am I Grateful for Today? _____

_____

_____

_____

How Did I Improve My Personal Rhythms For…?

Exercise: _____

Nutrition: _____

Sleep: _____

Date:_____

_____
_____
_____
_____
_____
_____
_____
_____
_____
_____
_____
_____
_____
_____
_____
_____
_____
_____
_____
_____
_____
_____
_____
_____
_____
_____
_____
_____
_____
_____

Date:_____   **Positive Comment:**_____

What Do I Desire To Improve In My Life Today? _____

_____

_____

_____

What Will I Do to Achieve the Imrovement? _____

_____

_____

_____

What Challenges Or Stressors Did I Face Today? _____

_____

_____

_____

What Did Or Will I Do To Rise To The Challenges? _____

_____

_____

_____

What Did I Learn from Today's Experiences? _____

_____

_____

_____

What Am I Grateful for Today? _____

_____

_____

_____

How Did I Improve My Personal Rhythms For…?

Exercise: _____

Nutrition: _____

Sleep: _____

Date:_____

Date:_____   **Positive Comment:**_____

What Do I Desire To Improve In My Life Today? _____

_____

_____

_____

What Will I Do to Achieve the Imrovement? _____

_____

_____

_____

What Challenges Or Stressors Did I Face Today? _____

_____

_____

_____

What Did Or Will I Do To Rise To The Challenges? _____

_____

_____

_____

What Did I Learn from Today's Experiences? _____

_____

_____

_____

What Am I Grateful for Today? _____

_____

_____

_____

How Did I Improve My Personal Rhythms For…?

*Exercise:*_____

*Nutrition:*_____

Sleep: _____

Date:_____

_____

_____

_____

_____

_____

_____

_____

_____

_____

_____

_____

_____

WEEKLY REVIEW

Areas where I felt successful this week

_____

_____

_____

Areas that I feel I need to focus on this week

_____

_____

_____

Positive personal comment for the week

_____

_____

_____

Most valuable lesson learned this week

_____

_____

_____

Date:_____   **Positive Comment:**_____

What Do I Desire To Improve In My Life Today? _____

_____

_____

_____

What Will I Do to Achieve the Imrovement? _____

_____

_____

_____

What Challenges Or Stressors Did I Face Today? _____

_____

_____

_____

What Did Or Will I Do To Rise To The Challenges? _____

_____

_____

_____

What Did I Learn from Today's Experiences? _____

_____

_____

_____

What Am I Grateful for Today? _____

_____

_____

_____

How Did I Improve My Personal Rhythms For…?

*Exercise:*_____

*Nutrition:*_____

Sleep: _____

Date:_____

_____
_____
_____
_____
_____
_____
_____
_____
_____
_____
_____
_____
_____
_____
_____
_____
_____
_____
_____
_____
_____
_____
_____
_____
_____
_____
_____
_____
_____
_____
_____
_____
_____
_____
_____

Date:_____   **Positive Comment:**_____

What Do I Desire To Improve In My Life Today? _____

_____

_____

_____

What Will I Do to Achieve the Imrovement? _____

_____

_____

_____

What Challenges Or Stressors Did I Face Today? _____

_____

_____

_____

What Did Or Will I Do To Rise To The Challenges? _____

_____

_____

_____

What Did I Learn from Today's Experiences? _____

_____

_____

_____

What Am I Grateful for Today? _____

_____

_____

_____

How Did I Improve My Personal Rhythms For…?

Exercise: _____

*Nutrition:*_____

Sleep: _____

Date:_____

_____

_____

_____

_____

_____

_____

_____

_____

_____

_____

_____

_____

_____

_____

_____

_____

_____

_____

_____

_____

_____

_____

_____

_____

_____

_____

_____

_____

_____

_____

_____

_____

_____

Date:_____   **Positive Comment:**_____

What Do I Desire To Improve In My Life Today? _____
_____
_____
_____

What Will I Do to Achieve the Imrovement? _____
_____
_____
_____

What Challenges Or Stressors Did I Face Today? _____
_____
_____
_____

What Did Or Will I Do To Rise To The Challenges? _____
_____
_____
_____

What Did I Learn from Today's Experiences? _____
_____
_____
_____

What Am I Grateful for Today? _____
_____
_____
_____

How Did I Improve My Personal Rhythms For…?

*Exercise:*_____

*Nutrition:*_____

Sleep: _____

Date:_____

Date:_____   **Positive Comment:**_____

What Do I Desire To Improve In My Life Today? _____
_____
_____
_____

What Will I Do to Achieve the Imrovement? _____
_____
_____
_____

What Challenges Or Stressors Did I Face Today? _____
_____
_____
_____

What Did Or Will I Do To Rise To The Challenges? _____
_____
_____
_____

What Did I Learn from Today's Experiences? _____
_____
_____
_____

What Am I Grateful for Today? _____
_____
_____
_____

How Did I Improve My Personal Rhythms For…?

Exercise: _____

*Nutrition:*_____

Sleep: _____

Date:_____

Date:_____   **Positive Comment:**_____

What Do I Desire To Improve In My Life Today? _____
_____
_____
_____

What Will I Do to Achieve the Imrovement? _____
_____
_____
_____

What Challenges Or Stressors Did I Face Today? _____
_____
_____
_____

What Did Or Will I Do To Rise To The Challenges? _____
_____
_____
_____

What Did I Learn from Today's Experiences? _____
_____
_____
_____

What Am I Grateful for Today? _____
_____
_____
_____

How Did I Improve My Personal Rhythms For...?

Exercise: _____

Nutrition: _____

Sleep: _____

Date:_____

_____
_____
_____
_____
_____
_____
_____
_____
_____
_____
_____
_____
_____
_____
_____
_____
_____
_____
_____
_____
_____
_____
_____
_____
_____
_____
_____
_____
_____
_____
_____
_____
_____

Date:_____ **Positive Comment:**_____

What Do I Desire To Improve In My Life Today? _____

_____

_____

_____

What Will I Do to Achieve the Imrovement? _____

_____

_____

_____

What Challenges Or Stressors Did I Face Today? _____

_____

_____

_____

What Did Or Will I Do To Rise To The Challenges? _____

_____

_____

_____

What Did I Learn from Today's Experiences? _____

_____

_____

_____

What Am I Grateful for Today? _____

_____

_____

_____

How Did I Improve My Personal Rhythms For…?

*Exercise:*_____

*Nutrition:*_____

Sleep: _____

Date:_____

_____

_____

_____

_____

_____

_____

_____

_____

_____

_____

_____

_____

WEEKLY REVIEW

Areas where I felt successful this week

_____

_____

_____

Areas that I feel I need to focus on this week

_____

_____

_____

Positive personal comment for the week

_____

_____

_____

Most valuable lesson learned this week

_____

_____

_____

Date:_____   **Positive Comment:**_____

What Do I Desire To Improve In My Life Today? _____
_____
_____
_____

What Will I Do to Achieve the Imrovement? _____
_____
_____
_____

What Challenges Or Stressors Did I Face Today? _____
_____
_____
_____

What Did Or Will I Do To Rise To The Challenges? _____
_____
_____
_____

What Did I Learn from Today's Experiences? _____
_____
_____
_____

What Am I Grateful for Today? _____
_____
_____
_____

How Did I Improve My Personal Rhythms For…?

Exercise: _____

Nutrition: _____

Sleep: _____

Date:_____

Date:_____   **Positive Comment:**_____

What Do I Desire To Improve In My Life Today? _____

_____

_____

_____

What Will I Do to Achieve the Imrovement? _____

_____

_____

_____

What Challenges Or Stressors Did I Face Today? _____

_____

_____

_____

What Did Or Will I Do To Rise To The Challenges? _____

_____

_____

_____

What Did I Learn from Today's Experiences? _____

_____

_____

_____

What Am I Grateful for Today? _____

_____

_____

_____

How Did I Improve My Personal Rhythms For…?

Exercise: _____

Nutrition: _____

Sleep: _____

Date:_____

Date:_____ **Positive Comment:**_____

What Do I Desire To Improve In My Life Today? _____
_____
_____
_____

What Will I Do to Achieve the Imrovement? _____
_____
_____
_____

What Challenges Or Stressors Did I Face Today? _____
_____
_____
_____

What Did Or Will I Do To Rise To The Challenges? _____
_____
_____
_____

What Did I Learn from Today's Experiences? _____
_____
_____
_____

What Am I Grateful for Today? _____
_____
_____
_____

How Did I Improve My Personal Rhythms For…?

*Exercise:*_____

*Nutrition:*_____

Sleep: _____

Date:_____

Date:_____ **Positive Comment:**_____

What Do I Desire To Improve In My Life Today? _____

_____

_____

_____

What Will I Do to Achieve the Imrovement? _____

_____

_____

_____

What Challenges Or Stressors Did I Face Today? _____

_____

_____

_____

What Did Or Will I Do To Rise To The Challenges? _____

_____

_____

_____

What Did I Learn from Today's Experiences? _____

_____

_____

_____

What Am I Grateful for Today? _____

_____

_____

_____

How Did I Improve My Personal Rhythms For…?

Exercise: _____

*Nutrition:*_____

Sleep: _____

Date:_____

Date:_____   **Positive Comment:**_____

What Do I Desire To Improve In My Life Today? _____

_____

_____

_____

What Will I Do to Achieve the Imrovement? _____

_____

_____

_____

What Challenges Or Stressors Did I Face Today? _____

_____

_____

_____

What Did Or Will I Do To Rise To The Challenges? _____

_____

_____

_____

What Did I Learn from Today's Experiences? _____

_____

_____

_____

What Am I Grateful for Today? _____

_____

_____

_____

How Did I Improve My Personal Rhythms For…?

*Exercise:*_____

*Nutrition:*_____

Sleep: _____

Date:_____

Date:_____   **Positive Comment:**_____

What Do I Desire To Improve In My Life Today? _____

_____

_____

_____

What Will I Do to Achieve the Imrovement? _____

_____

_____

_____

What Challenges Or Stressors Did I Face Today? _____

_____

_____

_____

What Did Or Will I Do To Rise To The Challenges? _____

_____

_____

_____

What Did I Learn from Today's Experiences? _____

_____

_____

_____

What Am I Grateful for Today? _____

_____

_____

_____

How Did I Improve My Personal Rhythms For…?

Exercise: _____

*Nutrition:*_____

Sleep: _____

Date:_____

_____

_____

_____

_____

_____

_____

_____

_____

_____

_____

_____

_____

_____

WEEKLY REVIEW

Areas where I felt successful this week

_____

_____

_____

Areas that I feel I need to focus on this week

_____

_____

_____

Positive personal comment for the week

_____

_____

_____

Most valuable lesson learned this week

_____

_____

_____

Date:_____   **Positive Comment:**_____

What Do I Desire To Improve In My Life Today? _____
_____
_____
_____

What Will I Do to Achieve the Imrovement? _____
_____
_____
_____

What Challenges Or Stressors Did I Face Today? _____
_____
_____
_____

What Did Or Will I Do To Rise To The Challenges? _____
_____
_____
_____

What Did I Learn from Today's Experiences? _____
_____
_____
_____

What Am I Grateful for Today? _____
_____
_____
_____

How Did I Improve My Personal Rhythms For…?

Exercise: _____

Nutrition: _____

Sleep: _____

Date:_____

Date:_____   **Positive Comment:**_____

What Do I Desire To Improve In My Life Today? _____

_____

_____

_____

What Will I Do to Achieve the Imrovement? _____

_____

_____

_____

What Challenges Or Stressors Did I Face Today? _____

_____

_____

_____

What Did Or Will I Do To Rise To The Challenges? _____

_____

_____

_____

What Did I Learn from Today's Experiences? _____

_____

_____

_____

What Am I Grateful for Today? _____

_____

_____

_____

How Did I Improve My Personal Rhythms For…?

Exercise: _____

*Nutrition:*_____

Sleep: _____

Date:_____

Date:_____   **Positive Comment:**_____

What Do I Desire To Improve In My Life Today? _____

_____

_____

_____

What Will I Do to Achieve the Imrovement? _____

_____

_____

_____

What Challenges Or Stressors Did I Face Today? _____

_____

_____

_____

What Did Or Will I Do To Rise To The Challenges? _____

_____

_____

_____

What Did I Learn from Today's Experiences? _____

_____

_____

_____

What Am I Grateful for Today? _____

_____

_____

_____

How Did I Improve My Personal Rhythms For…?

*Exercise:*_____

*Nutrition:*_____

Sleep: _____

Date:_____

Date:_____   **Positive Comment:**_____

What Do I Desire To Improve In My Life Today? _____
_____
_____
_____

What Will I Do to Achieve the Imrovement? _____
_____
_____
_____

What Challenges Or Stressors Did I Face Today? _____
_____
_____
_____

What Did Or Will I Do To Rise To The Challenges? _____
_____
_____
_____

What Did I Learn from Today's Experiences? _____
_____
_____
_____

What Am I Grateful for Today? _____
_____
_____
_____

How Did I Improve My Personal Rhythms For…?

*Exercise:*_____

*Nutrition:*_____

Sleep: _____

Date:_____

_____
_____
_____
_____
_____
_____
_____
_____
_____
_____
_____
_____
_____
_____
_____
_____
_____
_____
_____
_____
_____
_____
_____
_____
_____
_____
_____
_____
_____
_____
_____

Date:_____   **Positive Comment:**_____

What Do I Desire To Improve In My Life Today? _____

_____

_____

_____

What Will I Do to Achieve the Imrovement? _____

_____

_____

_____

What Challenges Or Stressors Did I Face Today? _____

_____

_____

_____

What Did Or Will I Do To Rise To The Challenges? _____

_____

_____

_____

What Did I Learn from Today's Experiences? _____

_____

_____

_____

What Am I Grateful for Today? _____

_____

_____

_____

How Did I Improve My Personal Rhythms For…?

Exercise: _____

*Nutrition:*_____

Sleep: _____

Date:_____

Date:_____   **Positive Comment:**_____

What Do I Desire To Improve In My Life Today? _____

_____

_____

_____

What Will I Do to Achieve the Imrovement? _____

_____

_____

_____

What Challenges Or Stressors Did I Face Today? _____

_____

_____

_____

What Did Or Will I Do To Rise To The Challenges? _____

_____

_____

_____

What Did I Learn from Today's Experiences? _____

_____

_____

_____

What Am I Grateful for Today? _____

_____

_____

_____

How Did I Improve My Personal Rhythms For...?

*Exercise:*_____

*Nutrition:*_____

Sleep: _____

Date:_____

_____
_____
_____
_____
_____
_____
_____
_____
_____
_____
_____
_____
_____

WEEKLY REVIEW

Areas where I felt successful this week

_____
_____
_____

Areas that I feel I need to focus on this week

_____
_____
_____

Positive personal comment for the week

_____
_____
_____

Most valuable lesson learned this week

_____
_____
_____

Date:_____ Positive Comment:_____

What Do I Desire To Improve In My Life Today? _____
_____
_____
_____

What Will I Do to Achieve the Imrovement? _____
_____
_____
_____

What Challenges Or Stressors Did I Face Today? _____
_____
_____
_____

What Did Or Will I Do To Rise To The Challenges? _____
_____
_____
_____

What Did I Learn from Today's Experiences? _____
_____
_____
_____

What Am I Grateful for Today? _____
_____
_____
_____

How Did I Improve My Personal Rhythms For...?

*Exercise:*_____

*Nutrition:*_____

Sleep: _____

Date:_____

_____
_____
_____
_____
_____
_____
_____
_____
_____
_____
_____
_____
_____
_____
_____
_____
_____
_____
_____
_____
_____
_____
_____
_____
_____
_____
_____
_____
_____
_____
_____

Date:_____   **Positive Comment:**_____

What Do I Desire To Improve In My Life Today? _____

_____

_____

_____

What Will I Do to Achieve the Imrovement? _____

_____

_____

_____

What Challenges Or Stressors Did I Face Today? _____

_____

_____

_____

What Did Or Will I Do To Rise To The Challenges? _____

_____

_____

_____

What Did I Learn from Today's Experiences? _____

_____

_____

_____

What Am I Grateful for Today? _____

_____

_____

_____

How Did I Improve My Personal Rhythms For…?

Exercise: _____

*Nutrition:*_____

Sleep: _____

Date:_____

_____

_____

_____

_____

_____

_____

_____

_____

_____

_____

_____

_____

_____

_____

_____

_____

_____

_____

_____

_____

_____

_____

_____

_____

_____

_____

_____

_____

_____

_____

_____

_____

_____

Date:_____   **Positive Comment:**_____

What Do I Desire To Improve In My Life Today? _____

_____

_____

_____

What Will I Do to Achieve the Imrovement? _____

_____

_____

_____

What Challenges Or Stressors Did I Face Today? _____

_____

_____

_____

What Did Or Will I Do To Rise To The Challenges? _____

_____

_____

_____

What Did I Learn from Today's Experiences? _____

_____

_____

_____

What Am I Grateful for Today? _____

_____

_____

_____

How Did I Improve My Personal Rhythms For…?

*Exercise:*_____

*Nutrition:*_____

Sleep: _____

Date:_____

_____
_____
_____
_____
_____
_____
_____
_____
_____
_____
_____
_____
_____
_____
_____
_____
_____
_____
_____
_____
_____
_____
_____
_____
_____
_____
_____
_____
_____
_____
_____
_____

Date:_____   **Positive Comment:**_____

What Do I Desire To Improve In My Life Today? _____
_____
_____
_____

What Will I Do to Achieve the Imrovement? _____
_____
_____
_____

What Challenges Or Stressors Did I Face Today? _____
_____
_____
_____

What Did Or Will I Do To Rise To The Challenges? _____
_____
_____
_____

What Did I Learn from Today's Experiences? _____
_____
_____
_____

What Am I Grateful for Today? _____
_____
_____
_____

How Did I Improve My Personal Rhythms For…?
Exercise: _____
*Nutrition:*_____
Sleep: _____

Date:_____

Date:_____   **Positive Comment:**_____

What Do I Desire To Improve In My Life Today? _____
_____
_____
_____

What Will I Do to Achieve the Imrovement? _____
_____
_____
_____

What Challenges Or Stressors Did I Face Today? _____
_____
_____
_____

What Did Or Will I Do To Rise To The Challenges? _____
_____
_____
_____

What Did I Learn from Today's Experiences? _____
_____
_____
_____

What Am I Grateful for Today? _____
_____
_____
_____

How Did I Improve My Personal Rhythms For…?

*Exercise:*_____

*Nutrition:*_____

Sleep: _____

Date:_____

_____
_____
_____
_____
_____
_____
_____
_____
_____
_____
_____
_____
_____
_____
_____
_____
_____
_____
_____
_____
_____
_____
_____
_____
_____
_____
_____
_____
_____
_____
_____

Date:_____ **Positive Comment:**_____

What Do I Desire To Improve In My Life Today? _____

_____

_____

_____

What Will I Do to Achieve the Imrovement? _____

_____

_____

_____

What Challenges Or Stressors Did I Face Today? _____

_____

_____

_____

What Did Or Will I Do To Rise To The Challenges? _____

_____

_____

_____

What Did I Learn from Today's Experiences? _____

_____

_____

_____

What Am I Grateful for Today? _____

_____

_____

_____

How Did I Improve My Personal Rhythms For…?

Exercise: _____

*Nutrition:*_____

Sleep: _____

Date:_____

_____

_____

_____

_____

_____

_____

_____

_____

_____

_____

_____

_____

WEEKLY REVIEW

Areas where I felt successful this week

_____

_____

_____

Areas that I feel I need to focus on this week

_____

_____

_____

Positive personal comment for the week

_____

_____

_____

Most valuable lesson learned this week

_____

_____

_____

Date:_____   **Positive Comment:**_____

What Do I Desire To Improve In My Life Today? _____
_____
_____
_____

What Will I Do to Achieve the Imrovement? _____
_____
_____
_____

What Challenges Or Stressors Did I Face Today? _____
_____
_____
_____

What Did Or Will I Do To Rise To The Challenges? _____
_____
_____
_____

What Did I Learn from Today's Experiences? _____
_____
_____
_____

What Am I Grateful for Today? _____
_____
_____
_____

How Did I Improve My Personal Rhythms For…?

*Exercise:*_____
*Nutrition:*_____
Sleep: _____

Date:_____

_____
_____
_____
_____
_____
_____
_____
_____
_____
_____
_____
_____
_____
_____
_____
_____
_____
_____
_____
_____
_____
_____
_____
_____
_____
_____
_____
_____
_____
_____

Date:_____   **Positive Comment:**_____

What Do I Desire To Improve In My Life Today? _____

_____

_____

_____

What Will I Do to Achieve the Imrovement? _____

_____

_____

_____

What Challenges Or Stressors Did I Face Today? _____

_____

_____

_____

What Did Or Will I Do To Rise To The Challenges? _____

_____

_____

_____

What Did I Learn from Today's Experiences? _____

_____

_____

_____

What Am I Grateful for Today? _____

_____

_____

_____

How Did I Improve My Personal Rhythms For…?

*Exercise:*_____

*Nutrition:*_____

Sleep: _____

Date:_____

_____
_____
_____
_____
_____
_____
_____
_____
_____
_____
_____
_____
_____
_____
_____
_____
_____
_____
_____
_____
_____
_____
_____
_____
_____
_____
_____
_____
_____
_____
_____
_____
_____

Date:_____   **Positive Comment:**_____

What Do I Desire To Improve In My Life Today? _____

_____

_____

_____

What Will I Do to Achieve the Imrovement? _____

_____

_____

_____

What Challenges Or Stressors Did I Face Today? _____

_____

_____

_____

What Did Or Will I Do To Rise To The Challenges? _____

_____

_____

_____

What Did I Learn from Today's Experiences? _____

_____

_____

_____

What Am I Grateful for Today? _____

_____

_____

_____

How Did I Improve My Personal Rhythms For…?

*Exercise:*_____

*Nutrition:*_____

Sleep: _____

Date:_____

Date:_____   **Positive Comment:**_____

What Do I Desire To Improve In My Life Today? _____

_____

_____

_____

What Will I Do to Achieve the Imrovement? _____

_____

_____

_____

What Challenges Or Stressors Did I Face Today? _____

_____

_____

_____

What Did Or Will I Do To Rise To The Challenges? _____

_____

_____

_____

What Did I Learn from Today's Experiences? _____

_____

_____

_____

What Am I Grateful for Today? _____

_____

_____

_____

How Did I Improve My Personal Rhythms For…?

*Exercise:*_____

*Nutrition:*_____

Sleep: _____

Date:_____